Price of Pride

Rex Southwell

Llumina
Press

ISBN: 978-1-60594-216-2 (PB)
      978-1-60594-217-9 (Ebook)

Printed in the United States of America by Llumina Press

Library of Congress Control Number: 2008910357

DEDICATION

The Price of Pride is dedicated first to my Lord Jesus Christ, who gave me life on this earth and the memory and strength in my later years to record it. Secondly, it is dedicated to my children and Christian friends, who recognize my human frailty, but see more the love and help from above. Appreciation is extended to family members who encouraged its writing, especially those who pushed me.

FOREWORD

In this sequel to *Tall Trees, Tall People*, I take the reader through the tumultuous twentieth century, which saw great wars and an economic depression beyond the comprehension of those not alive at the time, yet it also witnessed many great developments. When the century opened, the automobile was a novelty, the airplane existed only in imaginative minds, electricity was a fresh new possibility, and communications were primitive by today's standards. By the end of the century, the population of the United States had virtually tripled, roads had evolved from sand trails to great freeways, and air travel was available to anywhere in the world. Possibly greatest development of all was the computer.

Ordinary working people have much in common in their struggles, failures, and successes. In writing my memoirs, I believe it better to admit the failures and bring attention to the problems thus caused. While it is not pleasant to lay before my family and the reading public my character flaws, a reader will readily recognize that often, an inflated opinion of myself, a reticence to listen to the advice of others, and rebellion were causes of hardship for me and my family. Other times, my failures were simply results of mistakes, and I needed to remind myself that a mistake was not always a sin, but sin was always a mistake.

In spite of failures, God always opened a door through which I was able to step, resulting in an eventual good life for me and those he entrusted to my care. Many of those openings cannot be attributed to my efforts. I firmly believe they came as gifts from my Heavenly Father.

"Every good gift, and every perfect gift is from above, coming down from the Father of the heavenly lights, who does not change like shifting shadows." (James 1:17) For that, I am grateful and have been able to face life with an expectation of good. Because my wonderful wife's life was so closely intertwined with mine, I will write the story in the third person.

Table of Contents

Chapter 1

CHILDHOOD

Rex began life in a humble, unfinished house in Kalkaska County, Michigan, October 5, 1920. His father and mother shared a deep love of children and an even deeper love of Christ, giving him an environment far more beneficial than luxurious surroundings could have ever provided.

His parents, Grover and Grace, selected a hilltop in rural Michigan on which to build a home for their budding family, which included one young son, Harold, and another on the way. Living in a rented house a mile away, Grover and Grace struggled through the summers of 1918 and 1919 to build a place of their own. First, the stumps, brush, and debris were removed, leaving a space just large enough for a five-hundred-square-foot house and an accompanying yard. Three conveniently spaced young maple trees and one elm were saved to provide future shade. When they moved into the house in April 1920, it was barely more than a roof with walls, but it was their roof and their walls.

Grover dug up enough area around the rotting stumps to plant a garden, which provided most of their food through late summer and autumn. He then made what improvements he could inside the house so it was comfortable before winter. They were thankful to be in their own home before their second child was born. The interior of the house was divided into a kitchen, living room, and two bedrooms—one for Grover and Grace, and one for the children.

Each November, though reluctant to leave their new home, the family returned to the logging camp for Grover's winter work. Families in camp were provided a small, tarpaper-covered cabin for living quarters. Lumberjacks fortunate enough to be married returned to the dwellings each winter with their families to earn what would be the majority of their yearly income. For the first five winters of Rex's life, the family moved to the camp in the winter and returned to their farm home in the spring.

Rex and his brother knew nothing of their parents' struggles. Their home was filled with love, and their lives, while simple, were fulfilling. That his mother pumped their water from an outside well and the plumbing consisted of a slop jar[1] was not part of the small child's life. The fact that their father split wood for both the range[2] and the heating stove each night after they were asleep, yet usually left for work before the boys awoke in the morning, was likewise of no concern. Grover and Grace visualized the farm as a place where they would one day raise their children, and they worked happily toward that end.

The winter Rex was four, Frank and Myra Cunningham were camp cooks, and their son Jean, also four, became an instant companion for Harold and Rex. The boys were always together. Quite often, they played in the spacious cook shanty. When it was mealtime, the boys were all shooed over to Harold and Rex's limited quarters. The logging railroad, which ran between family housing and the cook shanty, was another place children could play without wading through the deep snow. The playground was not unsafe, however, because the company train came at nearly the same time each day. It arrived with empty flat cars and exchanged them for those loaded with logs.

When snow melted in the spring, puddles of water gathered on the frozen ground, and the children sailed their wood chip boats along the rails. For the children, it was exciting; for the parents, it was a constant battle to prevent their children from having soaked feet and legs in near-freezing weather.

Rex and Harold were disappointed when Jean did not return the following year. They missed their friend, but the new cook, Mr. Killarney, provided an interesting diversion for the children. Mr. Killarney intentionally cooked more pie or cake than the lumberjacks ate each day. He then set the remaining goodies out after the noon meal and invited the children who lived just across the tracks to help him dispose of the extras. Each noon, children lined the track, expectantly awaiting Mr. Killarney's call. There was always a treat for every child. Nobody left disappointed.

In September 1926, just prior to his sixth birthday, Rex and his brother Harold began their education in a little country schoolhouse, spending their first winter on the farm. Rural schools varied in size, but the Davis School usually had less than a dozen students. Typical of one-room country schools throughout rural America, young ladies who

---

[1] A ceramic pot under the bed which was emptied and washed each morning by his mother
[2] The cooking stove

had completed high school and a year of County Normal taught the children, even though many of the teachers were not yet twenty years old. Most, though not all, teachers read a portion of scripture each morning and taught the children to pledge allegiance to the flag.

On December 16, baby brother Bryce was born. Separated from Rex by six years, he would never have the close companionship Harold and Rex enjoyed, but he was a welcome addition to the family.

Harold and Rex now carried in the stove wood for their mother, and Harold filled the water pail each day when they returned from school. While they didn't entirely grasp why their mother needed their help, they were happy to have a little brother.

At school in winter, there was always fun in the snow. Younger children frolicked in the schoolyard, and older children who skied to school often slid down the big hill behind the barn at lunchtime. No one had a watch to keep track of time, and occasionally, when skiing was especially good, a late return to class brought reprimands from the teacher. The situation was never out of hand, at least in the children's eyes. In fall and spring, the teacher played softball with the children at recess and during the lunch hour.

Studies consisted of the three R's (reading, 'riting, and 'rithmatic), as well as geography, history, hygiene, and penmanship. On the first day of May each year, the teacher helped the children make little paper May Baskets to take to their parents. Wild flowers were abundant, and while walking home from school the children filled the baskets with mayflowers, adder tongues, "boys and girls,"[3] and occasionally an early blossoming trillium. In the summer months, they attended Sunday school in one of the school buildings in the area. Dedicated parents taught their children that God loved them from lessons furnished by the American Sunday School Union.

In 1929, Miss Duffy and Miss Lasore, two young ladies from Grand Rapids, stayed with Grover and Grace's family while conducting a two-week Bible school for the children in the area. Miss Lasore was blind, yet she communicated well with the children through song and Bible stories. The children seemed to sense their teacher's restriction and were unusually attentive.

---

[3] Dutchman's breeches

When Mr. Brown, from the American Sunday School Union, asked if the Southwells could provide living quarters for the two ladies, Grace had hesitated because Miss Lasore was blind. She was assured this would not be a problem because of the tender loving care provided by her associate. Such was the case. Miss Duffy also helped with housework in the evening while Miss Lasore entertained the children. She sang simple songs to Bryce, who was seated happily on her knee, unaware that Harold and Rex were also learning the songs. The entire Southwell family benefited greatly from the mission work of the ladies.

Grover cranked the Model T Ford for Grace each morning so she could drive their children and the teachers to the school. Each noon, Grover cranked the automobile again so his wife could pick them up. Harold, Rex, and many other children received meaningful instruction during these sessions. Whether Rex really understood the Bible message and placed his faith in Christ for forgiveness of sin at the time, or whether the teaching enabled his mother to lead him to his savior shortly thereafter, he really didn't know, but it was an important summer.

Through Grace's daily life and teachings, Harold and Rex placed their faith in Christ as their savior in their youth. Grace taught Bible verses to the children, and taught them to pray each night at bedtime:

Now I lay me down to sleep.
I pray the Lord, my soul to keep.
If I should die before I wake,
I pray the Lord my soul to take.

God bless Daddy and Momma,
Uncle Louis and Granddad,
Harold, Bryce, and myself,
In Jesus' name
Amen.

In the summer, the children worked on the farms. Rural families struggled to feed and clothe their children and the help was a necessity. Vacations from work were limited almost entirely to holidays.

Independence Day was always celebrated with enthusiasm. Flags were displayed on automobiles in every way imaginable. Grover even had a special radiator cap covered in flags. The sound of firecrackers echoed throughout the region as children and their families celebrated with gusto. Grover always made sure his sons had a reasonable supply of firecrackers. The boys would light the fuse and place a tin can over its top, then run back a safe distance and see how high the can would go.

For Rex's family, Sunday was a day of rest. The cows were milked, the livestock were fed, the barns were cleaned, wood was cut for the cook stove, and Grace cooked for the family. As much as possible, work was relegated to the other six days of the week.

The first ten years of Rex's life were truly ideal. Though his parents struggled in a rugged pioneer environment, the family was well provided with necessities and the comforts common to working people at that time. The 1920s were prosperous, and the children were showered with many small pleasures.

Chapter 2

TEEN YEARS

I n October 1930, the family reached two milestones: Rex achieved his tenth birthday and the Model T Ford finally reached the last of its useful days. Though it had served the Southwell family well, it was clearly obsolete. The engine required more work than it merited, so Grover replaced it with a shiny new Model A. Needless to say, the boys were delighted.

The following summer, the family often drove to one of the nearby lakes so the boys could swim. They'd pick up their friends, the Cunninghams, along the way. The two ladies sat in the back seat and the three boys rode on the running boards, loving every minute. By the time they arrived at the lake they'd be chilled, even on the warmest of evenings, and when they dove into the cool lake water, it felt abnormally warm. The ride home was even colder, making jackets a necessity.

In the winter of 1931, the Great Depression struck northern Michigan. Antrim Iron Company, the only large employer in the region, could no longer sell its products. When there was no more room to pile lumber, the sawmill shut down and the logging camp closed. When the railroad siding was clogged with pig iron, the blast furnace ceased operations. With no need for charcoal to purify the iron ore, the huge ovens that transformed the four-foot-long pieces of hardwood into charcoal and chemicals shut down. Everyone, including Grover's family, suffered through poverty like nothing they'd ever experienced. With no money to buy gasoline, the new Model A Ford sat idle in the garage, awaiting better days.

In spite of the conditions, life for Harold and Rex was never dull. When their day's work was finished, Harold and Rex would walk over the hill to Granddad's lake[4] and idly row for hours in their granddad's boat. The lake was as clear as crystal, and the boys would eagerly watch for the school of bass that often darted from under a big log near the small river outlet whenever they approached. Rex and Harold fished occasionally, but seldom caught anything. Grover said it was because

---

[4] Now officially named Southwell Lake

the fish could see every move they made. Catching fish wasn't important. The lake was their playground, and every hour passed together was a worthwhile endeavor.

Autumn signaled the beginning of one of the boys' favorite activities—hunting. They shared a single-barrel 410-gauge shotgun and in the evenings walked through the woods looking for ruffed grouse, which they called partridge, or just "pats," for short. Most of the time, when the birds were jumped and flew, neither Rex nor Harold ever saw them, but the sound of their wings on takeoff was unmistakable. Occasionally a pat stood its ground long enough for one of the boys to shoot it. The gun changed hands after one of the boys took a shot at a bird.

In winter, the boys enjoyed the challenge of hunting a different prey—snowshoe rabbits.[5] When they stumbled upon a fresh track, the boy with the shotgun waited while his brother followed the trail. The rabbits invariably made about a quarter-mile circle, coming back to where they had passed before. The boy following the track either barked like a dog or made some other sound so his brother knew where he was. This doubled as a signal that the rabbit was getting near and a safety precaution to avoid an accidental shooting. As the sound came closer, tension grew because the rabbit was usually hopping along not far ahead of the boy. While the climax of the chase was a shot at the rabbit, Rex enjoyed the tracking almost as much as the shooting because the rabbit often employed a number of tricks to hide its trail, and the challenge of outsmarting it was exhilarating.

In the autumn of 1933, Harold began high school in Mancelona, seven miles away. The following year, Rex began his high school studies. Through the fall and spring months, the boys drove the car seven miles to school, but in winter, they parked the car at the nearest plowed road, one and a half miles away. The boys would walk from home to the car in the morning, drive to school and back, and then walk the mile and a half home each afternoon. Though Grover and Grace had no money for gasoline, they arranged to pay Clyde Smith at the Sunoco station with produce.

When he began high school, Rex was still quite small and wore glasses, which was uncommon for boys at the time. The girl behind

---

[5] Technically, these were snowshoe hares, not snowshoe rabbits, but local people seldom used that term.

him in study hall immediately dubbed him "Popeye."[6] Rex was humiliated and made little effort to be friendly with his classmates. He did, however, make great efforts to improve his skill at baseball, which became his obsession throughout high school.

Cherishing the chance to practice and improve his skills, Rex attended every practice and game. When storm clouds threatened to cancel either activity, he would stare out the window, wishing for the clouds to disperse. Rex knew he played well and yearned for an opportunity. His brother was on the varsity team, and Rex saw no reason why he shouldn't be, but the coach obviously did not share his opinion.

Finally, when Rex was sixteen, he experienced a phenomenal growth spurt, and in the spring of his junior year, his dream of joining the varsity baseball team was realized. As his outward appearance changed, Rex found his attitude changing, because for the first time, Rex found acceptance with his peers.

Rex's first game was against Gaylord. Mancelona was one run behind in the final inning when Rex drove a double down the left-field line and a base runner scored to tie the game. The next batter doubled, and Rex crossed the plate and scored the winning run. Very few times was he the hero, but the accolades he received that afternoon would remain in his memory for life.

In the winter of 1935, Antrim Iron Company resumed production. Grover worked once more skidding logs and hauling four-foot pieces of wood to accessible roads, where Antrim Iron Company crews picked it up. When spring arrived, the family began attending church in Excelsior, and the pastor scheduled a baptism for mid-summer. Grace asked her sons if they wished to be baptized, but neither had been taught the reason for baptism, and they hesitated to answer. She explained that baptism represented the death, burial, and resurrection of Jesus and was a public testimony that a person had accepted Christ as his savior. She asked if they had such faith in Christ, and when they answered in the affirmative, she suggested they consider baptism. By Sunday, both boys had decided to be baptized.

The baptism was held at Crawford Lake, about one mile from the church. Several young people were baptized, including their friends, Loren

---

[6] The pugilistic sailor of the same name was a popular comic strip character at the time.

and Sybil Armstrong. The service at Crawford Lake by Rev. O. B. Little would be forever special in Rex's memory.

That summer, the family moved temporarily to Chestonia, where Grover obtained employment skidding logs. Rex and Harold were hired on as sawyers and paid six cents per log. The trees were short, and most had only one log. Most days they averaged twenty-five logs, which provided each with an income of seventy-five cents per day. At a time when most men were happy to find work at a dollar a day, it was a good income that allowed them to purchase new clothes for school and heavy clothing for winter.

In August, Grace wanted to take the family to visit her father at Hubbard Lake, near Alpena. Wilmar, her father, was seventy years old, and Grace wanted the family to see him again while he was still living. This posed two problems. First, her brother Louis, who lived in Antrim County, had no automobile. Second, her sister Emma had died in 1918, leaving behind two babies, Ralph and Earl,[7] who now lived in Mancelona. Grace thought it important that her brother, nephews, and immediate family visit Grandpa Williams one last time, but there wasn't enough room in the car.

During the five years of financial hardship, she had been unable to fulfill this wish, but Grover found a way. He borrowed a trailer for the boys and laid straw in the bottom for their comfort. Now they could invite Ralph and Earl to share the journey with them. The four boys enjoyed the fresh air, and the adults sat comfortably inside. Grover's ingenuity allowed the whole family to visit Wilmar Williams and his wife, Anna.[8]

Harold graduated in the spring of 1937. Being younger, Rex had been deprived of the privilege of driving to school for three years and chaffed at the delay. Finally, in the fall of 1937, his opportunity to drive to school came. The old Model A Ford had served faithfully, but it was at the end of its days. Grover needed something different for Rex to drive.

Grover's cousin and close friend, Henry Klomparens, accepted a 1924 Franklin as payment on a long-overdue plumbing bill and asked Grover if he wanted it for Rex. The car had been driven very little be-

---

[7] Grace and Grover cared for both boys temporarily until their father remarried.

[8] This was Wilmer's second wife. His first wife was named Anna as well.

fore the owner died. His wife had never driven it, so the old sedan had remained in the garage for more than ten years and looked new. The aged lady was happy to give the car to Henry to cover the thirty-five-dollar bill.

Automobiles had changed greatly in thirteen years, and the Franklin was definitely vintage. While antiques were not yet the rage, its age made it an attraction. The horn made an intermittent "Ah-Ah-Ah-Ah," making Rex's arrival at school unmistakable. Colleagues often wanted a ride in the Franklin, and he was more popular than ever.

After a long lapse during the Depression, in 1937, football was restored as a sport in the Mancelona School. The equipment was resurrected from the lockers. It was in dismal shape. Rex loved the game and the contact. One of his teammates reminded him years later that he had at least one black eye after every game. After one game, he had a pair of shiners.

Once, Rex's shoulder pads broke. Rather than lose playing time, he took them off, threw them to the sideline, and finished the game without them. At the end of the game, the coach found out and was not timid in expressing his disapproval. Rex never did such a foolish thing again.

Rex was a nominal student. He never took a book home to study, but he loved reading, as long as he didn't have to master the content. In his senior year, he dedicated himself more to his schoolwork. That year, he earned three A's and one B and graduated with a three-point average.

Rex wanted to attend college, and Mr. Flynn, the agriculture teacher, found someone to provide him with a tuition and books scholarship to Michigan State. While the offer was generous, he would have to leave home with the clothes on his back and not one dollar in his pocket. That, plus the need to find full-time work, and facing the big world alone loomed like an ominous mountain before him. Upon graduation in 1938, Rex wondered at the word "Commencement." It made no sense. He had attained!

Chapter 3

EMPLOYMENT

R ex graduated from Mancelona High School in the spring of 1938. The depression of the 1930s had taxed the country's economy severely. Employment was virtually non-existent in the area, so Rex was pleased when he was offered a summer-long job on the Dunlap Dairy Farm. Ira and Esther Dunlap, members of the church Rex attended with his family, offered him thirty dollars a month, plus board and lodging. Rex accepted the job immediately.

Rex worked hard during the days and spent his nights with the Dunlap family. The only change to his daily schedule was on Sunday, a day of rest on the Dunlap farm. After taking care of the livestock, he attended church with both the Dunlaps and his own family. He then returned to his family's home for dinner and enjoyed the afternoon with them before returning to the farm. He was employed, content with his labors, and more importantly, he was happy; life with the Dunlaps was much like life at home. The love he was accustomed to receiving was bestowed on Max and Gordon, their two young sons. With two children clamoring for attention, Rex's evenings were never boring.

Eventually, the harvest ended, and Rex was no longer needed. He had been promised work only through the summer, so he departed the Dunlap farm to join the ranks of other young men looking for employment. Rex found an advertisement for the Radio-Electronics-Television School in Detroit, which promised work with the airlines for their graduates. Tuition was a hundred and sixty dollars, and most of the course could be completed by correspondence, allowing Rex to move at his own pace. Rex had saved a hundred of the hundred and twenty dollars he had been paid for the summer's work, and he seized the opportunity, despite his lack of interest in radio.

The written lessons interested Rex greatly, though he never used the equipment provided to build a crystal radio set and testing equipment. The tests he had to pass were written, and Rex didn't understand the need for practical knowledge. His studies progressed well until midwinter. When Rex had no money to order additional courses, his career in radio came to a screeching halt. Not much later, in March 1939,

13

Glenn Cotton and son, prominent local farmers, began selling Allis Chalmers farm equipment and needed help assembling the machinery. Where some saw fortuitous coincidence, Rex saw the workings of his Lord's providence; he applied immediately.

Glenn Cotton's daughter-in-law, Phoebe Dunlap, knew Rex from his work at the Dunlap farm and recommended him for the job. The advantage of hiring single men was that room and board could be more easily provided in exchange for help with barn chores mornings, and Rex could dedicate himself to the work fully.

When the job was offered, Rex hesitated. His heart was set on working for the airlines, but since he could not afford more lessons, he accepted the opportunity. With barn chores morning and night, and work in town during the day, his hours were long, but he was glad to be employed. Nine dollars a week was better than the thirty a month he had received the previous summer, and he could resume his radio lessons, though slowly. In November, he purchased material for a workbench and began work on the crystal set and testing equipment.

Saturday morning, when Rex drove to Mancelona to buy the materials, his father drove to Kalkaska to summon a doctor. Bryce had fallen ill on Friday and missed school, but he had become seriously ill overnight. When Rex returned home, his mother met him at the door.

"Be very quiet," she said. "Dr. Sargent is here. Bryce has pneumonia and a hundred and six-degree fever. The doctor says he has very little chance."

The diagnosis was a shock to the entire family. Bryce had always been a strong, healthy boy and to get sick so quickly and die was beyond comprehension. Nevertheless, on Sunday morning, Bryce breathed his last and passed on to his home in heaven.

The loss was devastating to Rex and Harold's parents. Their life was their children. They had lost their only daughter when she was ten days old; now Bryce was gone. However, in spite of their grief, all three men were back at work before the week ended.

Assembling farm machinery interested and challenged Rex. It amazed him that a piece of farm equipment could materialize from a pile of disorganized parts. The only machines that needed no assembly were the tractors.

Since farmers bought equipment only when it was needed, there was no machinery to assemble in wintertime, so Rex moved to the potato warehouse. Often, he and another driver delivered truckloads of potatoes to the market in Detroit, a difficult assignment. After spending all day sorting and bagging potatoes, they left Kalkaska at seven p.m., drove two hundred and fifty miles south, and reached the market in Detroit at four a.m. As soon as the potatoes were unloaded, they drove to Logan, Ohio, some fifty miles southeast of Columbus, where they loaded the truck with coal for the return trip. If they were unable to reach the mine in Ohio before the tipple closed for the night, they rented a room and loaded the truck in the morning; otherwise, they loaded the truck in the evening and made the trip to Kalkaska in the night, each man sleeping in turn in the cab.

The demand for farm equipment seemed insatiable, and the Cottons established a sub-agency in Lake City, a prosperous farm community thirty miles to the south. On May 1, 1940, Glenn Cotton asked Rex to manage the satellite in Lake City. He offered the use of an automobile and gasoline, twelve dollars per week salary, and a one-percent commission on all sales. He added that, when sales warranted, Rex would be rewarded accordingly. Rex barely heard the financial offer or wondered how he would live on his own with such a meager income; he would have his own wheels! At nineteen, it was a big deal.

The Lake City branch was not one to warrant much attention; it was only a small garage behind a gas station. The inconspicuous driveway beside the station likewise drew little notice, but a bright orange sign by the road that proclaimed "Allis Chalmers" proved hard to ignore, and the customers began coming.

In the garage, Rex had a vast quantity of booklets explaining the superiority of the equipment he sold; he could furnish any tool a farmer wished to buy. While it would have been nice to have a tractor sitting at the entrance, the Cottons brought a manure spreader, hardly the grand picture Rex held in his mind.

Upon his arrival in town, Rex drove through the small town searching for board and room, but found only one sign, which declared that a room, but not board, was available. Glenn Hause, who operated his own garage and welding shop in Lake City, stopped to welcome Rex to the area. Glenn had done some work for Cottons and had met Rex before. When Glenn learned of Rex's need for board and room he said, "It's possible my mother-in-law would take you in." Glenn brought Rex to his mother-in-law's home and introduced him.

Mrs. McVicar hesitated. After a while, she said, "We have an extra bedroom. I guess you can stay here. I will have to charge you $4.50 a week for room and board." She went on to say her husband worked for the state highway, and casually mentioned they had a son and daughter.

When Mr. McVicar and Rex came from work that evening, Mrs. McVicar called them to supper. They were at the table when an attractive young lady walked in unannounced. She was their daughter Evelyn. Rex was shocked, as the connection dawned on him. The daughter Mrs. McVicar had mentioned was not a child.

For some time, communication between Evelyn and Rex was limited. Evelyn was busy at the Dahlquist store, and Rex was equally busy making contacts to sell farm machinery. Not many farmers stopped at the garage behind the station, and Rex made very few sales. He began visiting the surrounding farms in the evening, distributing literature and touting the value and price of Allis Chalmers tractors. He communicated well with the struggling farmers and encouraged them to purchase additional equipment to help with their work.

During this time, employment became more available in nearby cities, encouraging farm boys to leave the community to look for other work. The resulting need for farm equipment to replace them increased, and Rex was more than willing to help farmers choose the best equipment.

One pleasant evening in early June, Rex had an appointment to visit a likely prospect for a tractor sale, and he asked Evelyn if she would care to go along for the ride. She agreed. Neither Rex nor Evelyn could find suitable topics of conversation. Briefly, they mentioned their respective jobs, but much of the ride was spent in a rather awkward silence. On their return to Lake City, they drove past an abandoned farmhouse. The yard was covered with beautiful lilacs. Rex stopped and asked Evelyn to wait while he picked some for her. The wooden stems were hard to break, but Rex, like everyone else at the time, carried a pocketknife and cut a beautiful bouquet for his companion, who seemed pleased to receive them. The lilacs' lovely perfume filled the car, and upon impulse, Rex drove back to the yard and cut more, which he placed over the visors. Conversation relaxed as he and his companion returned to her home.

Evelyn began to accompany Rex on some of his sales trips, and the evenings became more and more pleasant. When the lilacs were gone, Rex found rose bushes at abandoned farms to replace them. He kept flowers above the visors all summer. As autumn approached, Rex found more potential buyers. Rex's treats for Evelyn amounted to an occasional evening at the local theater followed by a dish of ice cream or a milk shake. He had very little money, but he had a car and he had gasoline. It was a very pleasant summer.

In October, the Cottons closed the outlet in Lake City for the winter, and Rex returned to harvesting and marketing potatoes. He lived at home and was allowed continued use of the automobile; however, gas was no longer provided.

The daily grind of sorting, bagging, and trucking potatoes kept Rex very busy, but he soon realized Evelyn had become much more than a pleasant companion. The summer had been relaxed and pleasant, more so than any other of Rex's life. He began to realize he couldn't live without Evelyn, and whenever possible, he drove to Lake City in the evenings. For weeks, Rex planned to share New Year's Eve with her, but on December 31, he was stuck in southern Ohio peddling a truckload of unsold potatoes. Rex couldn't bear the possibility of Evelyn thinking he'd forgotten her, so he sent a telegram.

All winter, the yearning continued. On Easter Sunday, 1941, Rex asked Evelyn to be his wife, though both knew they could not live on his present income. Evelyn agreed to marry him when it became possible, and Rex turned his attention to studying radio at every possible moment, though few such moments presented themselves.

In April, Rex returned to Lake City selling farm machinery, and once again, Mrs. McVicar provided room and board. Sales were brisk, keeping Rex busy and giving him a slight boost in income from his commission. Rex sold two tractors and related machinery in April, an enormous sale at the time. He should have been happy, but he was miserable; he wanted to be married, but Evelyn insisted he be able to support her first.

Rex waited for word from the Cottons about a salary increase, as he was selling a large amount of machinery and improving their contacts in the region, but none came. He tried to study in the evenings, but all he could think about was Evelyn. On Memorial Day weekend, for the third time, it just happened that Glenn Hause offered Rex a marvelous opportunity.

Glenn had moved to Detroit with his family, and he was very profitably employed. Welders were in great demand as the country struggled to expand the manufacture of war equipment. Glenn could pick his job. When he understood Rex's dilemma, Glenn made an offer. "The gas station across from our apartment needs a man to work nights. You could work there and board with us."

Rex was excited for the opportunity; he could work nights and attend radio school. Staying in his room and studying, knowing Evelyn was just downstairs, required more discipline than Rex possessed. He had to complete some of his studies at the Detroit school before he could graduate, and the opportunity was too good to give up.

The Cottons had not kept their promise of raising his wages when sales increased, even though he had worked hard to meet his end of their agreement. He felt he owed them nothing more and prepared to leave gracefully. Rex listed the articles of machinery he had sold that had not yet been delivered, and gave the locations for their delivery. He gave directions for pending sales. He cleaned the garage, put every detail in order, and submitted a bill for expenses. Saturday night, Rex gave all the pertinent information to Glenn Cotton, handed him keys to the automobile he had been driving, and told him he was leaving.

Glenn was furious. "You can't do that!" he exclaimed.

Rex was as polite as possible, though such a response was unexpected. Mr. Cotton offered to make new financial arrangements, but Rex had made his decision. Surprisingly, the Cottons did not send another employee to continue operating the agency, and the Lake City branch ceased to exist.

Chapter 4

EVELYN

On November 28, 1919, Evelyn was born in a farmhouse seven miles east of Lake City, Michigan, the youngest of five siblings. It was a struggle for her parents to provide for two sons and three daughters, but the children loved the carefree country life. Evelyn remembered her eldest sister being unable to refrain from stepping into the fresh puddles of cow manure, giggling as the warm semifluid mixture squeezed between her toes. Though Evelyn did not share her sister's amusement in that respect, she derived great pleasure from the occasional ride on the back of one docile old cow. Marian and Mike, the two eldest siblings, set her on the back of the cow when they drove the herd to the barn for milking.

Another of Evelyn's fondest memories was of her Grandpa Sheldon, Mrs. McVicar's father, who dwelled on a homestead a few miles north of their home. On Sunday afternoons, the family gathered under a huge oak tree in the front yard and made ice cream. A metal can was filled with eggs, cream, milk, and a little flavoring and placed in a special wooden tub equipped with a crank to turn a set of paddles inside the can. Grandpa took a piece of ice from the sawdust in the icehouse, put it in a burlap bag, and broke it into little pieces with the side of his ax.

Grandpa had spent many hours the previous winter cutting ice from the nearby lake and storing it in the icehouse, but the delight of the boys and girls gathered under the tree was Grandpa's reward. Ice chips and salt were placed in the wooden tub around the metal container, and for what seemed like ages to a small girl, the children turned the handle and stirred the contents. After about a half hour, the ice cream was properly frozen. It didn't take the family long to consume the six quarts of ice cream. After a hug and kiss from Grandpa and Grandma, the McVicar family, tired but happy, rode home on the farm wagon.

In 1925, the family moved to a house only two miles from Lake City, where school was more accessible. Mr. McVicar found employment with the State Highway Department. One stormy December day, Mrs. McVicar told the children, "We're coming to town today, and when school's out, you can ride home with us on the sleigh." The children hurried from school, anticipating the ride home, but their parents were not there. Evelyn's brother Bill, eight years old, was impatient and unpredictable. In spite of blizzard conditions, Bill took his little sister by the hand and walked home. The snow was not yet very deep, and they took the normal shortcut across the fields.

When Mr. and Mrs. McVicar arrived at school a short time later, their three older children were patiently waiting, but Bill and Evelyn were nowhere in sight. Neither school officials nor family found any trace of the young children. Finally, the frantic parents and three older children hurried home. No one they met on the road had seen the children.

When they arrived at their house, Bill had added wood to the fire and smoke was coming from the chimney. Evelyn and Bill sat comfortably by the big living room stove. Poor Bill could not understand why his parents were upset. The following year, the family moved into town to a house only a few blocks from school.

Will was determined that his family would have milk and butter, so he rented a shed and a small pasture at the edge of town to care for the cow until the children were grown. In winter, Evelyn went fishing with her father in a fish shanty on Lake Missaukee. She enjoyed pulling the string to move the decoy, and occasionally, her father speared a large pike. In summer, Will took his children to Goose Lake. He propped cane poles over crotched sticks stuck in the sandy beach and built a small bonfire. The children roasted hot dogs and marshmallows in the embers while watching the fishing poles. Whether Evelyn caught a fish didn't matter, and the evenings with her father became treasured memories. Lake Missaukee's beautiful beach was only a few blocks from the McVicar home and was a playground for children in the small town. Evelyn loved the water and was an excellent swimmer.

When Evelyn was in high school, the Barrens family moved to Lake City. Their younger daughter Barbara shared classes with Evelyn and became her closest friend. The children were often together, and after a time, Evelyn grew attached to Barbara's brother Morris. The feeling appeared mutual. The Barrens family attended church regularly, and though religion had never been part of Evelyn's life, she began attending church with her new friends. Morris invited Evelyn to accompany him to evangelistic meetings at a church in Cadillac. It was at these meetings that Evelyn learned Christ had died for her, and she accepted him as her savior.

After two years, the Barrens family moved away. For Evelyn, it was a great loss. She not only lost Barbara's Christian companionship, she had become very fond of Morris. Though Evelyn and Barbara remained close friends, and Evelyn was bridesmaid at Barbara's wedding, Morris moved out of her life. However, her relationship with the Barrens family introduced her to a friend that would never leave her—Christ Jesus. None of Evelyn's family or friends accompanied her, but she found her way to church weekly, and her devotion to Christ never faltered. Truly, he was a friend that never failed.

Evelyn finished high school in May 1939. The day the final tests were given was exceptionally warm and beautiful. It was a day to be at the state park, taking the first spring dip in the icy waters of Lake Missaukee. Several of Evelyn's friends succumbed to the temptation, and Evelyn joined them. The school superintendent took a dim view of their absence and declared that none of them would be allowed to graduate. Fortunately, after intercessions from the parents, the superintendent relented. Evelyn always felt fortunate that H.G. Bacon, whose father was chairman of the school board, was one of the truants. The teachers reluctantly donated a day of their vacation and allowed the students to write their final tests so they could go to commencement with their classmates.

Through her junior high and senior high years, Evelyn waited tables at a local restaurant. When she graduated and applied for work at a convenience store, she was immediately hired. Mr. Dahlquist operated a small chain of five-and-dime stores, and the Lake City store had recently opened.

One spring day the following year, Evelyn's mother came to the store and said, "Glenn brought a man to see me who needs a place to stay. He'll probably be there when you come home from work, and I didn't want you to be surprised."

Evelyn was disturbed. Her mother had made baked goods for a local restaurant for years and had recently been forced to quit because of her blood pressure.

"You can't take on a boarder. You just quit working at the restaurant!" she proclaimed.

"I did, though," her mother replied, then turned and walked away.

Alice Patterson, a young lady working with Evelyn, said, "I'll come up tonight, and we'll look him over." Soon the girls were busy with customers, and the intruder was forgotten. When Evelyn came home later and saw a young man at the table, she remembered what her mother had said and ran to the bathroom to contain her embarrassment.

Evelyn was civil to Rex, but she did not believe her mother should be caring for an additional person. Still, he was here, and Evelyn did what she could to help her mother with the work. Evelyn had been deeply hurt when Morris moved away and was not interested in male companionship. The feeling appeared to be mutual. Rex often left in the evenings to visit local farms, so their relationship stayed civil, and nothing more.

It did intrigue Evelyn that when Rex came to the house, he was usually whistling and happy. When he asked if she would care to ride with him one evening, she thought to herself, "Why not? It could be fun."

Rex was polite, though not a conversationalist, and Evelyn was determined not to be overly friendly. After all, she barely knew the man and did not wish to give him the wrong impression. On their return to Lake City, Rex saw a patch of lilacs by an abandoned house and suddenly stopped and turned in. Evelyn sat in the car and watched as Rex cut a bouquet of lilacs. He didn't say anything; he just shrugged his shoulders and passed them through the window.

Rex cut more flowers and fastened them to the visor. Finally, he said, "They smell good, don't they?"

A few days later, Rex invited Evelyn to ride with him again. She didn't talk much, but she smiled. Several times in the following weeks, she accompanied Rex on his sales trips and when one evening he asked if she would accompany him to a show at the local theater, she again thought, "Why not?"

When they came to the ticket window, Rex fumbled in his pocket, and then sheepishly said, "I don't have my billfold. Can I borrow money for the tickets?"

Evelyn paid for the tickets, wondering if he were really that hard up for money, or if he was just stingy. When they returned home, Rex gave her back the money. Evelyn was relieved.

More and more often, Rex asked Evelyn to accompany him on evening drives, and she wondered, "Does he really care about me? Do I want him to care?"

When Rex left for the winter, Evelyn missed the evenings with him and was pleased that he often came to visit on Saturday evenings. Easter was drawing near, and one Saturday night, Rex sat beside Evelyn looking through the Sears catalogue. It was something they often did, but tonight Rex seemed to be on a mission. He turned to jewelry, chose an engagement ring, and asked, "If I buy you one of these, will you wear it?"

Evelyn wasn't really surprised at the proposal, but his way of expressing his love was unusual. She considered the possibility and replied, "I would be happy to wear the ring, Rex, but we aren't able to be married."

Rex understood. He was anxious to be married, but Evelyn was right. He could not support a wife. He had wanted to finish the radio course, but the pleasures of the present had kept him from his goal. They agreed Evelyn would accept the ring, and Rex would find more-profitable employment, though how or when, they didn't know.

Rex returned to Lake City in April, and though he stayed at Evelyn's home, the joy was not the same as the year before. Rex wanted to be married, but it just was not possible. When Evelyn's sister Mary and her husband told Rex there was work in Detroit, and offered him the opportunity to stay with them, she was both pained and relieved. She missed her fiancé, but it was better this way.

Evelyn received virtually no communication from Rex, but Mary said, "He's working night and day. Don't worry about it."

In August, Rex came to see Evelyn, and his feelings had not diminished with his absence. Rex assured her that he had almost finished his studies and they should be able to be married in the winter; Evelyn was relieved. In October, Rex called. He had passed the test and received his commercial radio license. American Airlines had promised him employment, but he had to brush up on his typing. They were excited; soon they would be married.

However, their plans were dashed on December 7, when the Japanese bombed Pearl Harbor. Rex was twenty-one, and young men were needed for military service. Marriage had to wait. The future was uncertain, but Evelyn had faith there would be one for her and the one she loved.

Chapter 5

DETROIT

G lenn Hause often spoke glowingly of the opportunities available in the city. In Detroit, he had moved from one employer to another several times. The war in Europe called for more and more equipment, and the United States was becoming the arsenal for the Allies. The U.S. was also rearming, and new employees were needed at factories in Detroit.

Glenn and Mary invited Rex to live with them in Detroit, which would give him an opportunity to finish school, get a better job, and be married. Leaving beautiful northern Michigan for a congested city seemed a sacrifice to Rex, but his parents had always looked ahead rather than dwelling on the past, and he was prepared to do the same. Rex was very grateful.

Glenn's apartment was on the corner of La Fayette and Trumbull, just six blocks south of Tiger Stadium. The apartment was in an older, less desirable section of the city, but nothing better was available. Mary was willing to combat the cockroaches and the environment. Her family lived where Glenn had work, and they were together. It was enough.

Diagonally across the street from Glenn and Mary's apartment was the City Service gasoline station where Rex could work. The station blended well with the community; it was nothing to brag about. Glenn introduced Rex to Jim Howard, the station owner, and he was offered work seven p.m. to seven a.m. six nights a week. Night work was exactly what Rex needed. In Lake City, there had been a choice between studying and spending evenings with Evelyn, and he had been unable to make the harder choice.

In retrospect, Rex was pleased with the rewards from his employment with the Cottons. The work had been exciting. He had been a successful salesman. Of greater significance, he had met Evelyn. To say Rex was grateful would hardly be true. He was pleased with the results, true, but gratitude would come much later in life.

Rex's weekly salary was twenty-five dollars, and if his performance on the job warranted it, his salary would be increased. Twenty-five dollars a week sounded attractive. Room and board with Glenn and Mary was eight-fifty week, but what was left over was substantially more than in Lake City.

Rex attended radio school from nine to twelve a.m., Monday through Friday. A second-class commercial radio license was required to be a radio operator for the rapidly expanding commercial airlines. Passing the test required considerable knowledge of both alternating and direct current, development and control of specific frequencies for local or long distance transmission of signals, and knowledge of the methods and equipment necessary to implant sound in radio waves for transmission and produce the sound through headphones or speakers. While it sounded complicated and difficult, Rex knew he could master the material. His work and study allowed for little free time and only a few hours of sleep each afternoon, but he tackled both with vigor.

The school was at 4709 Woodward Avenue, six miles east of the Hauses' residence. Bus transportation was available, but the bus routes were a problem. Rex boarded a bus, but it went only two blocks before turning north. Rex was puzzled, but got off at the first stop, walked back to Lafayette Avenue, and boarded the next bus.

When that bus also turned north before reaching Woodward Avenue, Rex was not happy, to say the least, and got off again. The third bus he boarded took him up Woodward Avenue to the radio school.

On the return trip, Rex boarded a bus, but when it turned before reaching Lafayette Ave., Rex lost all faith in Detroit's bus system. "I need to find another means of transportation," he thought.

Fortunately, the second bus Rex boarded continued on to Lafayette Street and past his apartment. Even more fortunately, by conversing with a passenger in the adjacent seat, Rex learned what longer-term city dwellers already knew. Each bus had a sign above the windshield listing its destination. Maybe he could get to school by bus after all.

Rex struggled to maintain his studies and work. He could sleep all day on Saturday and Sunday if the heat was not too oppressive, but there was little breeze through the downtown apartment and sleep did not come easily. One morning, when Jim checked the pumps, Rex was fifteen dollars short, and he had no explanation for the shortfall. Jim knew Rex was struggling to work and study, and he concluded that Rex had fallen asleep and someone had taken some gasoline for which he did not pay.

The station was open twenty-four hours, but in the wee hours of the morning, very few customers stopped. Jim said, "If you have trouble staying awake, turn off the pumps, pull your chair up, and put your feet against the door. If someone wants gas, they'll wake you up." Occasionally, toward morning, when all was quiet, Rex followed his advice, and there were no more shortages.

Working nights in the older section of downtown Detroit was educational for a boy from rural northern Michigan. There were an abundance of nightspots in the area and quite often, someone would appear, beaten and battered, at the station late in the night. Though usually drunk, the man would want to call the police and report being robbed. It was not unusual for him to request a nickel so he could use the pay phone. The calls usually followed the same pattern: the man had no sooner left a bar than he was assaulted and robbed.

One night when responding to a call, a weary policeman gruffly advised, "If you'd take your paycheck home to your wife instead of spending it on that babe in the bar, this wouldn't happen to you." A statement that brought to mind the difficulties alcohol had afflicted on Rex's own grandfather, Tuden.

The office for Teamsters Union Local 299 was on Trumbull Avenue, just a half-block south of the station where Rex worked. There were eight business agents, all very friendly. One was Mr. Bowers and the other was Mr. Jimmy Hoffa. Mr. Hoffa later became well known as the teamsters' president.

When the business agents' cars needed gasoline or servicing, they parked them at the station and walked to the office. It was a time of extensive union activity, and since an agent could be needed at any time, each expected his automobile to always be ready for use. Jim Howard was happy to insure that. Rex or another attendant filled the car with gasoline, checked the oil and water, cleaned the car, and parked it behind the station. The service was free, but the union customers were dependable and provided a substantial portion of Jim's business.

A local trucking company provided another major source of income for the station. Each morning, a group of trucks lined the driveway before heading out on the road. Rex worked feverishly for about a half-hour before going home each morning to get them on their way. It went quickly because the drivers just signed a payment slip, and the company cared for the bills later.

Riding city buses to school was time consuming, so Rex decided to purchase a car. An automobile would save time and give him another hour of sleep each day, but that was only part of the reason he wanted his own transportation. After having had the use of a car for more than a year, he missed the luxury.

With very little money for a down payment, Rex found little worth buying. Jim Howard came to the rescue. He offered Rex a very good 1936 Plymouth for a hundred and eighty-five dollars. Rex gave Jim fifty dollars for a down payment, and Jim deducted ten dollars from Rex's salary each week for the balance.

In mid-August, Jim gave Rex a week's paid vacation and increased his wages to thirty-five dollars a week. Jim's generous vacation offer enabled Rex to visit Evelyn and his parents up north. It was a welcome break, and Rex was pleased, but again, to say he was grateful would have given him undue credit. That Tuesday night, while Rex was on vacation, the station was held up. The attendant at the time, whom Rex remembers only as Slim, was still in his teens, but he reacted maturely, and the robbers only took money. No one was hurt.

Barney Lempke worked days at the station and seemed to be a man of some importance. One day, he gave Rex some literature from a group called the Technocrats, an organization he thought Rex might be interested in joining. After examining the material, Rex exclaimed, "That's communist!" Barney shrugged his shoulders, and they discussed the Technocrats no further.

Youth gangs roamed the streets. The Purple gang and the Howard Street gang ruled the area. Late one evening, when Glenn was returning from work, a youth from one of the gangs jumped onto his car, hanging on the driver's door. Glenn hit the young man's hands with a club he carried in the car, and the youth let go and jumped off.

Unfortunately, this occurred a few blocks from Glenn's home, and the gang followed the car to Jim Howard's station, where Glenn took refuge. The youth came in the station and beat Glenn severely about the face. When Rex tried to phone the police, other members of the gang advised him not to get involved. Little by little, Rex was learning about city life and human nature.

Chapter 6

DECEMBER 7, 1941

I t was a struggle to attend classes through the hot summer months, but Rex persevered, and in October, he completed the radio school courses. Only a second-class commercial license was required for airline work, but the instructor told Rex he was qualified to take the test for a first-class license. If he passed, it would qualify him for work at any radio station, or with an airline company.

The test was not too difficult, and two weeks later, the anxiously awaited results arrived. Enclosed in the envelope from the local office of the Federal Communications Commission was the first-class license. Attached to the license was an anonymous note. "If you would like a good job, go to the 45th floor of the Penobscot Building in Cadillac Square." Cadillac Square was in downtown Detroit.

There was not the slightest suggestion as to what Rex would find when he got there, but as soon as possible, he hurried downtown. At the indicated location, he discovered the home office of a new radio station—W45D. It was one of the earliest FM stations, and it later became known as WWJ-FM. His studies had included frequency modulation, so this was indeed the opportunity of a lifetime. Rex's hopes soared.

After carefully examining Rex's qualifications, the station manager frowned. "I'd like to hire you," the manager said, "but there is a problem. You're twenty-one years old. I'll just get you trained for the job, and you'll be called for military service."

Because of the steadily deteriorating relations with Japan, and the possibility of the US being involved in the war in Europe, a military draft had been instituted in August. Rex didn't see that as a problem and replied, "Yes, I quite probably will serve, but I'll come back as soon as my duty is over."

"That's what I'm afraid of." The manager went on to explain that he did not want to have to release another employee when Rex returned from service.

Though disappointed by not getting the job at the radio station, Rex went on to the Detroit Metro Airport and applied for work at American Airlines, his original objective. American Airlines had helped finance

Douglas Aircraft in the development of the DC-3, and they were the only airline with a fleet entirely composed of the marvelous new aircraft. They were also the leading commercial carrier in the nation.

The man in charge of American Airlines Personnel looked at Rex's license. "The airline needs radio operators," he said, "but all our messages are copied with a typewriter, and we require a typing proficiency of fifty words per minute."

Rex hesitated. He had taken typing in high school but hadn't typed for nearly two years. "I'll need to practice," he said, and he headed back to his room at the Hause home.

Rex was dejected, but he did not give up. He rented a typewriter and began typing a couple of hours each day. Fifty words a minute was not difficult; minimizing errors was not as easy.

Thanksgiving Day arrived, and Rex celebrated with Glenn, Mary, and their two girls, Marilyn and Shirley. Mary had prepared a bountiful feast, and there were many things for which to be thankful. Work was plentiful. The depression that had plagued the nation for so many years was over, and Rex believed he was nearly ready for the typing test. If he passed, he would be able to get the job and support a wife. He was eager to marry Evelyn, so it was truly a day for rejoicing and thanksgiving. Ten days later, on a Sunday afternoon, Rex awoke to an alarming announcement. The Japanese had bombed Honolulu.

Much had been said about the tension between the United States and Japan, so Rex was not overly surprised a bombing had taken place. But Hawaii? He said, "You must mean Manila." An attack on the Philippines would have surprised no one, but an attack on the Hawaiian Islands was unthinkable.

For some time, the extent of the devastation of Pearl Harbor was kept from the public. The government feared telling the Japanese that the islands were almost defenseless. Marriage was again forced into the background. Rex immediately went to enlist for pilot training in the air force. He wanted to fly a P-40 fighter plane.

Rex was devastated when neither the air force nor the navy would accept him because his vision was 20-30, but he only wore glasses because he had a small astigmatism, and he was not ready to give up his dream of flying a fighter plane. Rex returned to developing his typing proficiency while deciding what his next move would be. His eyes weren't bad; they were just not quite good enough to be a cadet.

One day, Rex asked a doctor who was a regular customer if he knew any way to circumvent the eye test. The doctor replied, "You're too old to enlist as a cadet anyway."

Shocked, Rex asked, "How old do you think I am?"

"About thirty," the doctor replied.

It had been a hard year, but Rex was amazed that he looked that old. He'd turned twenty-one only two months earlier. The doctor suggested Rex not wear his glasses for a month and try again to pass the eye exam. It seemed a good suggestion. However, in early January, he again failed the eye exam for both the air force and navy cadet programs.

Rex had diligently kept at his typing practice, and he returned to Detroit Metro Airport to take American Airline's typing test. It wasn't really a test. The station manager watched him type half a page and was satisfied. Rex's previous dejection turned to enthusiasm when he was given a pass to fly to the home office at La Guardia Field, New York City. All potential employees were sent to La Guardia for interviews. He was hired and began training with five other newly hired radio operators in early February.

In late February, the *Normandy*, a large French luxury liner, was burned at a dock in New York harbor. Felix Citkowitcz, a trainee who lived in New York, borrowed an automobile and took Rex and his other classmates to see the fire.

While firemen battled the blaze, a long line of police kept cars moving. They got only a brief glimpse of a gigantic liner lying on its side and smoke clouds billowing upward. It later was revealed that fire was the work of arsonists trying to prevent the ship from being used for troop transport. At that time, Japanese troops were attacking the Philippines. The Marines at Wake Island had surrendered after their aircraft were destroyed and most of the garrison had been killed. All the news from the battlefront was distressing.

After a six-week training period, Rex received a work assignment at Midway Field in Chicago, one of American Airlines' flight control centers. Rex's journey had taken many unexpected turns, but he finally had the job he'd been working toward for two long years.

Rex still wanted to enter military service, but he remembered the struggle he'd had in obtaining satisfactory employment. Anyone who worked six months on a job before entering the military would be guaranteed the job when the war was over. Because there was no indication that the war would end soon, Rex decided to take the deal.

After working for six months, Rex enlisted in the navy. His radio experience enabled him to enlist as a second-class petty officer, and he was ecstatic. He passed the physical and expected to begin boot camp immediately, but hit another roadblock. The enlistment officer told him American Airlines had obtained a deferment for him as an essential employee, and the navy could not accept him.

No one had told him he was deferred. Neither the airline nor the draft board would cancel the deferment, so no branch of the military could accept him. Rex remembered his mother saying, "Man proposes, but God disposes." It was a lesson he was slowly learning.

Rex chaffed. His plans always seemed thwarted. His work was interesting, but his life was not. The routine of eating alone each day for lunch, either in the little sandwich shop or in the Greek restaurant on the corner of 63rd and Cicero, became monotonous. He had no close friends in Chicago and that left him alone when he was off work.

One night, Rex awoke and thought, "I can't get into the navy. I have the job I wanted. Maybe Evelyn will marry me now."

When the idea was proposed, Evelyn hesitated. They had been engaged for a year and a half, but she and Rex had seen each other only twice in the last eighteen months. It was like marrying a stranger. Fortunately, however, Evelyn soon agreed. Marriage arrangements were difficult in wartime. They both needed blood tests done in Michigan. Satisfactory results had to be submitted with the application for a marriage license.

Rex purchased train tickets to Detroit one evening, returning the next day so he wouldn't miss work. Both his and Evelyn's blood tests were accepted, but the license could only be obtained in Kalkaska County in northern Michigan, where Rex was born.

Reluctantly, Evelyn agreed to go to Kalkaska and buy the license. She didn't like the implication inherent in those days of the lady obtaining the license, but she overcame her reticence. Under the circumstances, the wedding was far from the romantic event every young lady desires, but after nearly two years of engagement, Evelyn and Rex were happy to join their lives together. On January 17, 1943, they were married at Evelyn's parent's home in Lake City. The love they had felt so keenly when they were together before would once again return.

Evelyn's brother Bill and his wife Pauline were the attendants, and Rev. O.B. Little performed the ceremony. Beyond that, only Rex and Evelyn's parents and two other ladies were present. They faced an uncertain future, but they happily faced it together.

TOGETHER

One dreams of taking his bride to a beautiful home, carrying her over the threshold, and saying, "It's all yours." Rex had much less to offer. Housing was almost unobtainable in wartime Chicago, but Rex had found an apartment on the second floor of a private house. It consisted of a bedroom, bath, small living room, and a kitchen on the ground floor that was shared with the homeowners. The humble circumstances did little to dampen Rex and Evelyn's joy; they were happy to finally be together.

The house was only a half-mile from where Rex worked, allowing him to walk to his job, and freeing up the car for Evelyn's use. Evelyn had no friendships in the area and little interest in driving around Chicago. Since Rex's income allowed for little recreational spending, it was not long before Evelyn became bored sitting alone in their little apartment all day.

Just a block from their home, the Cracker Jack Company was packing K-rations for the army and more workers were needed. One night after the evening meal, Evelyn took Rex's hand and said softly, "Rex, I sit here all day doing nothing while you are away. I could go help pack K-rations at Cracker Jack."

Rex was horrified. He had struggled to get a good job so he could care for a wife. Now she wanted to go to work. The thought was humiliating. The wartime economy necessitated that many women be employed outside the home, but it had always been expected in both the McVicar and Southwell families that a husband should support his wife.

The next evening, Evelyn approached Rex again. "I get bored, Rex. I have never just sat around doing nothing. I'd much rather be working. We will still have time together."

Rex considered life from his wife's perspective and understood. She had no garden to weed, no children to care for, and no labor to fill the long hours while he was away at work. He wouldn't want to sit all day, either, yet the thought of his wife working wounded his pride. He had married Evelyn and wanted to care for her. Still, if Evelyn wanted to work, he wouldn't try to stop her.

Evelyn began folding boxes all day on an assembly line; her fingers swelled and sleep became difficult, but occupying her time with a meaningful activity gave a sense of purpose to her days. On days when he was home alone, Rex found the absence of his wife unbearable. One such day, he called Cracker Jack and asked that they send Evelyn home. He gave no reason. When the message was brought to Evelyn, an older lady advised, "If your husband wants you, you go! He will find someone else." Evelyn came home, and they enjoyed an afternoon on the town, but wanting to be a responsible employee, she asked Rex not to repeat the call.

Rex's own duties rotated through three shifts: days, evenings, and midnights. The changes in his shifts made it difficult to schedule regular activities, and one Sunday morning he and Evelyn realized neither had been to a church service for some time.

The Cicero Bible Church, with its fiery young pastor Billy McCarroll, was only two miles up Cicero Avenue from Rex and Evelyn's home. Someone suggested they would find the services interesting. Pastor McCarroll taught that salvation came only through accepting Christ's death as a payment for one's sin and as a substitute for one's own eternal death. That was what Rex and Evelyn believed, and they attended the Cicero Bible Church through the spring months.

Pastor McCarroll was an eloquent speaker, but Rex and Evelyn felt lost in the large church. Personal friendships eluded them, and they found a small bible church only a short drive west in La Grange. This smaller community church provided both the ministry and companionship they desired, and their attendance and service continued until they were forced to move away.

Rex had no great interest in telegraphy,[9] but soon after being hired, he learned that radio operators qualified for both radiotelephone and radiotelegraph received twenty-five dollars more each month than those who could only perform one of these functions. This was due largely to the fact that all reservations and cargo messages were by telegraph, while contacts with planes were made by radiotelephone. Thus, he began working diligently to become proficient as a radio-telegrapher.

Even after he was married, Rex stayed an hour after work each day and practiced copying radiotelegraph messages. By midsummer 1943,

[9] The practice of transmitting communications through Morse Code

he was able to send and receive messages at the required thirty words per minute, and he received the promised raise. Life became a little easier for the young couple.

In 1944, the pool of young men available for the draft was fast diminishing, and the federal government was forced to cancel many deferments. The FCC reduced the requirement to be a radiotelephone operator to a restricted permit, which covered only communication laws that could be learned in the space of a few hours. Young ladies began replacing men, who were needed in the military.

Simultaneously, the teletype rapidly replaced radiotelegraph as a means of communication between airports. Messages were now sent at sixty words per minute, rather than thirty-five by radiotelegraph, and required only a skilled typist. Since his license was no longer required, Rex was notified to report to his draft board in Michigan for a physical and was inducted into the armed forces on April 20, 1944. Rex and Evelyn's time together, more than a year, had been a privilege few their age enjoyed during the war.

Chapter 8

SEPARATED

W ith mixed feelings, Rex and Evelyn loaded their meager be-
longings in the car and drove to the home of Rex's parents in
Mancelona, Michigan. Young wives were being separated
from their husbands daily, and Evelyn was not surprised to become one
of many. Her brother Bill was in the air force and had been separated
from his wife Pauline for more than a year. Now it was Evelyn's turn.
When Rex and five other draftees boarded the train in Kalkaska to report for duty in Fort Sheridan, Illinois, Evelyn drove to Pontiac, where
she had been offered work with her sister.

Evelyn's eldest sister, Marian, and her husband Bill Lotan had purchased a half-interest in Manning's Produce and Fish Market. Evelyn's
knowledge of marketing and constant smile made her a welcome addition to the staff. Evelyn's parents had also moved to Pontiac soon after
her wedding. Will, her father, worked in the market and Mrs. McVicar[10] cared for Bill and Marian's house and family

While reluctant to leave his happy life with Evelyn, Rex truly desired to be in the armed forces. He was disappointed that he couldn't
pick where he was to serve, but he was enthusiastic about being a part
of the war effort. Military stories had loomed large in his life, and he
finally had the opportunity to create his own. Rex soon learned, however, that the road to glory had many obstacles.

New arrivals in Ft. Sheridan were immediately fitted with uniforms,
or more often than not, simply provided uniforms. They also received
multiple shots, which gave many recruits, including Rex, a fever. His
first day in uniform, Rex was assigned to kitchen police (KP) duty. He
and the other recruits began work at four a.m. and worked constantly
until the kitchen was cleaned at eight p.m. His fever seemed to add
even more hours to the long first day.

Next was classification, where each person's qualifications were
noted and usually ignored. A recruit generally was sent where he was

---

[10] While almost everyone called Evelyn's father Will, no one ever called Mrs. McVicar by her first name, Florence.

needed the most, and being able-bodied was valued more than knowledge or skill. Occasionally, a recruit was assigned where his past
experience and education were utilized. Rex, fortunately, was one of
those cases.

In early 1942, there was a critical need for air transport, but all military personnel were urgently needed for combat assignments. To meet
the need, C.R. Smith, president of American Airlines, was called into
service, commissioned as a brigadier general, and given the responsibility of establishing an air transport command (ATC). General Smith
immediately solicited volunteers from the airlines to form the nucleus
of this command. The original group was made up of civilians, but they
were given officer uniforms so they would have military status in case
they were captured.

General Smith then commandeered approximately half the planes
from each of the commercial airlines. That was the origin of the ATC,
which became a prominent part of the army air force.[11] More experienced airline personnel were urgently needed in the ATC, so all airline
employees were told, if and when they were drafted, they were to send
a telegram to General Smith, who would then request they be assigned
to the ATC.

Most new soldiers left Ft. Sheridan in groups, but Rex was given a
train ticket to travel alone to Las Vegas, New Mexico. Detailed information was never given to recruits, and Rex was concerned. Las Vegas
was in Nevada, he knew, but apparently, the U.S. Army was not aware
of that.

The train ride was hardly a pleasure trip. It was stiflingly hot crossing Kansas, but toward the evening of the second day, Rex saw the
peaks of two large mountains in the distance. All through the afternoon,
the peaks remained in view, but they never seemed to grow closer.
Thankfully, when he awoke to the jostling of the railroad car in the
middle of the night, they were passing through rugged mountain ter-
rain, which he later learned was Raton Pass, on the Colorado-New
Mexico border.

At mid-morning, Rex and a half-dozen other recruits disembarked
in the small, but very beautiful community of Las Vegas, which was in
New Mexico, after all. Las Vegas was the training camp for the New

---

[11] In July 1947, the U.S. Air Force was separated from the U.S. Army, becoming an
independent branch of the military

Mexico National Guard. The small, but adequate, camp was an excellent facility for ATC personnel to receive basic training.

The first instruction given was on military courtesy. Enlisted men were taught to salute officers, who could be recognized by the emblems of rank on their shoulders. Enlisted men wore stripes, if they had earned any, on their upper arms. Rex was delighted to be in uniform.

His flight[12] received extensive training with the .22 caliber target rifle, the .30 caliber Springfield rifle and the .30 caliber carbine. Rex had a great time because rifles and shotguns had been a love of his life, and now someone else was paying for the ammunition. The Thompson sub-machine gun and its cheaper counterpart were demonstrated, and the troops were allotted twenty-five rounds to familiarize themselves with each. Twenty-five rounds hardly made a burst with the Thompson, but the cheaper counterpart, nicknamed a "grease gun," fired much more slowly, which was more practical for the inexperienced.

Recruits were taught how to use a gas mask and forced to inhale a small amount of a gas that left them choking for a time. They were taught to pitch a shelter half, in which two soldiers each set up a canvas from their backpack to form a small tent. Differing from the rugged basic training most troops endured, ATC inductees were given very little close order drill or harsh workouts.

The unit was forced to go on only one bivouac, or camp-out. One dark night, the flight was ordered out on the mountainside, where they set up their shelter halves. Around midnight, they were attacked with smoke bombs. Afterwards, they picked up their equipment and marched back to the mess hall for a late-night snack. Ground forces might have smirked at the treatment, but no one in Rex's flight had any objection to the lighter duty.

In June, Rex finished basic training and eagerly awaited assignment. He received classification as a radio operator and was eager to begin flying. Radio operators in planes worked exclusively with radio-telegraph, which operated at only sixteen words per minute. Rex was more than qualified, but it was reasonable, due to the need to use a hand key, rather than the faster semi-automatic "bug."

Throughout the summer, the men fell out for roll call each morning and a list was read for those receiving assignment. Rex looked forward

---

[12] The air force designation for a group

to the day his name would be read from the list, but the months passed, and he waited in vain. Each morning, those whose names were not called were sent to finish KP or the duties of those who had received shipping orders. Much to his chagrin, Rex became a highly skilled KP.

In October, Rex and thirty-eight others who had never received assignment were told there was no need for their specialty and they were being sent to Mill's Field, San Francisco. There they would learn to load and secure cargo on aircraft, after which they would be assigned to duty. After four weeks of training, the flight of thirty-nine airmen, thoroughly dejected, were given a fifteen-day furlough and instructed to return to Mather Field, Sacramento, an aerial port of embarkation. Finally, the former airline employees were assured, assignment was near.

After returning from furlough, the same thirty-nine airmen became more disgruntled as they languished for four weeks, still with no assignment. They were then sent to Kearns Field, Utah; it seemed the ATC had no need for former airline employees. For men who considered themselves valuable for their background and skills, this was an especially bitter pill. General Smith had requested their assignment to the ATC, but now they were unneeded.

Morale hit bottom, and they remained in Utah through the holidays. An occasional assignment consisted of KP or guard duty. At times, they practiced close order drill or "policed the field," which meant walking abreast across the grounds, picking up cigarette butts or other discarded items.

Unfortunately for everyone involved, a carefree, irresponsible young man known as Shadda became the undesignated leader of his restless companions. One day, the flight was being marched to chow at noon and Shadda, who always managed to be first in line, turned into the back door of the mess hall, and the entire flight followed, leaving the sergeant marching on alone. When the sergeant reached the street corner and ordered, "Right turn," he was embarrassed to find no troops behind him. Needless to say, this did not sit well with the sergeant or the officer of the day. That evening, the flight was marched to the mess hall, where they listened to an extensive discourse on military courtesy. Thankfully, no other punishment was administered.

January is very cold in northern Utah, and the barracks at Kearns Field were single boarded with coal-fired stoves intermittently spaced throughout the building for heat. A separate barracks was designated for those assigned to KP, but no preparation was made to keep the barracks warm. Each evening when KP assignments were posted on the bulletin board, the men on the list were ordered to move with their bedrolls to the KP barracks where the CQ (charge of quarters) would come to call them for duty at four a.m. the next morning.

Rex's entire flight was assigned to KP the same day. Since their own barracks was as near the headquarters building as the KP barracks, the men thought the CQ could call them from their own warm quarters just as easily. Rex was designated to make the request. The response was not just negative; Rex also received a royal chewing out for even making the suggestion. Resigned to his fate, Rex rolled up his bedding, went to the KP barracks, built a roaring fire, and retired in a bunk nearby.

Others in the flight saw no reason for all of them to suffer, so they asked Rex to wake them in the morning when the CQ called and retired to their quarters. In the morning, the CQ, after seeing no one in the KP barracks after a quick glance, went to the other barracks and woke the flight. Roll call was taken, and Rex was missing. The CQ was furious. Fortunately, his fellow airmen told him where Rex was.

Rex was awakened and informed that he was off KP for the day, but he considered it wise to volunteer, and he worked through the day with the rest of the flight. When the duty roster was posted for the next day, Rex was assigned to weapons cleaning, a goof-off detail, but everyone else in his flight was back on KP. There was much grumbling, but they did spend the night in the KP barracks.

KP at a large base is hard work, and at mid-afternoon, the flight staged a short sit-down strike. It wasn't long before an officer appeared and the flight was marched to the base theater. There, the officer of the day read the Articles of War. When the troops realized their action could be considered treasonous, they became diligent workmen.

In early January, the flight was sent to Camp Anza, near Los Angeles. They embarked, along with four thousand regular troops, a large contingent of officers, and some Red Cross workers, on the troop ship J.H. McRay. The date was January 11, 1945. The airmen were pleased to be going somewhere. Anywhere, they thought, would be better than Kearns Field.

Rex's flight stood in line through most of the night as they awaited their turn to board the ship. There had been much grumbling about the inadequacies of the Red Cross, but Rex was pleased. Throughout the night, Red Cross workers moved up and down the line with hot coffee, sandwiches, and donuts. The consideration was more valuable to him than the food.

After several days aboard ship, the captain in charge of the flight called a meeting and said. "I can't tell you where we're going, but I can tell you it's a good deal." Since they'd left from the West Coast, Rex and the others spent their days speculating on their destination; it had to be somewhere in the Pacific Theater. Two troop ships traveled together, avoiding land to prevent the Japanese from learning their whereabouts. At the end of three weeks, they tied up in the harbor at Melbourne, Australia, but no one was allowed to disembark.

After taking on supplies, the ships continued another three weeks and finally tied up in the Ganges River at Calcutta, India. While the food had been reasonably good for the first three weeks, it consisted mostly of mutton and beans for the second leg of the journey. The last day on ship, they were given beans for breakfast, chili for dinner, and beans for supper.

The following morning, the close-knit group from Kearns Field began a slow train ride from the dock to Kanchrapara, a staging area in the jungle. At night, hyenas howled at the edge of the camp, and jackals ran through the tents searching for scraps of food. The men wondered about the good deal. If this was good, they were thankful for it, but they felt sorry for those with the bad deal.

Not realizing they had became known as "rebellious," the men were surprised to learn they would be dispersed throughout the India China Division. After nearly a year, Rex was content to do almost anything. If he couldn't fly, he could at least load cargo.

Chapter 9

ASSIGNMENT

All the ground supply routes to China had been cut off by the Japanese, and American and Chinese forces there were in danger of imminent collapse due to a shortage of food and ammunition. The objective of the ATC in India was to fly as many supplies as possible to the troops in China.

Supplies arrived in Calcutta by ship, and they were moved by rail or riverboat up the Bramaputra River Valley to the Assam Province in northeast India, to be delivered to a number of American airbases built beside the river. Once the supplies reached those bases, the ATC took charge of them. Crews flew over the Himalayan Mountains, called "the Hump," to Kunming, China every day.

Rex arrived at Dum Dum Airbase near Calcutta, India in late February 1945. It was a desirable assignment, at least compared to other bases in the CBI (China/Burma/India) theater. Dum Dum was a previously established British airport from which both British and American transport planes operated. Emergency supplies were distributed from Dum Dum throughout the entire theater of the India China Division.

As was customary with any new arrival, Rex was interviewed by the classification officer. Though he had been advised that the ATC had no need for more radio operators, he maintained a vain hope that somewhere he would find an opportunity to fly. When the officer opened Rex's records, Rex asked, "Could you use a radio operator?"

For what seemed an unreasonably long time, the officer said nothing and examined Rex's file. Finally, after adding something to the file, the officer indicated they definitely did need radio operators. Rex would soon discover just how severe the need was.

Rex was moved to a tent with other radio operators. Each tent contained two beds on each side and one across the back. The beds were equipped with a mosquito net. The edges were tucked under the mattress and were effective in protecting from malaria-carrying mosquitoes.

It was expected that each airman would care for his own space, but a bahra[13] could be hired very reasonably. Each airman paid the bahra

---

[13] A local servant

five rupees (US $1.50) per month, making them the highest-paid locals on the base. The tent was always clean, and the bed net was put down at sundown, except on holidays. No one ever knew the religion of our bahra, Babu, but when either the Hindus or Muslims had a holiday, Babu had a day off.

Gurka[14] guards patrolled the area to prevent theft. Occasionally, they killed a cobra that strayed into camp from the nearby jungle. That added benefit became more significant to Rex when a guard killed a large one across the ditch from his tent. A canopy above the tent served quite effectively as an insulator. The tents were much more comfortable than the bamboo "bashas" provided for the men at the bases up the Assam Valley. A latrine at the end of the tent area provided showers and drinking water, both from the same source, as well as facilities for their physical needs. Most of the year, it was very comfortable for showers, and Rex soon became accustomed to drinking tepid and even warm water.

Rex's name had immediately been placed on the flight schedule. His only indoctrination consisted of being shown the equipment and given the key for decoding five letter groups into messages.[15] Regulations limited each airman to a hundred hours per month in the air, and men were to be rotated (sent home) when they reached a thousand hours. Actually, men were still on duty with far more than a thousand hours, and everyone was flying more than a hundred hours a month. Each month from April until the end of the war, Rex's flying time exceeded a hundred and twenty-five hours, once even reaching as high as a hundred and forty-eight hours. Even then, Rex was content. Though

---

[14] One of the many ethnic groups in India

[15] Communication between planes en route and between planes and airports was done using the radiotelegraph, a system using dots and dashes to represent letters. This technology predated communication by radiotelephone by many years. While this was time consuming, it was dependable and easily understood by trained operators. Airlines and the army air force used International Morse code. For example, the letter A was represented by a dot and a dash (. –), B a dash and three dots (– . . .), C a dash, dot, dash, dot (– . – .), etc.

To speed communication, a code was developed using five letter groups. The location of a letter within the group indicated what it represented. SXTNE, for example, represented Dum Dum airfield (SX), thunderstorms (T), and wind direction from the northeast (NE). Various five-letter groups provided other information.

he would have appreciated more sleep between flights, the need of the soldiers who depended on his flights sustained him.

In March and April, Allied troops were heavily engaged with Japanese forces in Central Burma. Pursuit aircraft, or fighter aircraft, based near the mountainous jungle between India and Burma made daily forays over these mountains to strafe the Japanese. Many of Rex's early flights carried 50-caliber ammunition for these planes.

When the Central Burma campaign ended, there was no diminishing of flights. Critically needed repair parts were flown from Dum Dum to bases throughout the area. Planes from Dum Dum carried mail to bases in what are now India, Pakistan, Bangladesh, and the Island of Ceylon (Sri Lanka). On one flight, Rex's crew flew five tons of paper money, printed in England, into Kunming and then on to Chungking, Generalissimo Chiang Kai-sheck's headquarters.

The Chinese nationalist government under Chiang Kai-shek was desperately fighting the communists in the north, under Mao Tse-tung, and the Japanese in the south. Because of this great pressure, governmental functions had practically ceased to exist, even to the extent of being able to print their own currency.

Rex's crew flew up the Assam Valley many times, and each time, Rex hoped to see the peak of Mt. Everest, but the peak was always immersed in clouds. Thunderstorms were a constant threat through the monsoon season from April to September, but the need for supplies was so great that the planes flew regardless of weather. A few storms were so severe and the vertical currents so strong that the downdraft pulled at the seat belt on the legs, keeping one in the seat. The sudden change to an updraft was often strong enough to disorient even veteran fliers. On many occasions, Rex expected the wings to be ripped off the plane, yet they always somehow held up.

Both the Douglas C-47 and the Curtis Commando C-46 planes were used at Dum Dum. These twin-engine workhorses flew with a pilot, copilot, and radio operator (RO). Ships with four engines, the C-87, C-109, and C-54 carried a crew of four, with the added crewmember being a flight engineer.

When these planes arrived at their destination, the pilot and copilot went to operations and made out a flight plan for the return trip. On the C-47 and C-46, the radio operator stayed by the plane to guard and refuel it. When the gas truck came to the plane on Rex's first flight, he had no inkling where the gas tanks were filled. The smiling truck driver assured Rex that he had helped many new RO's, surprised to be expected to fulfill the duty of a flight engineer while the officers were doing the paperwork and getting lunch.

After a few hungry days, Rex learned he could draw K-rations when he left for a flight if he wished. They would be his sole sustenance until he returned to his home base. The biscuits in the K-rations were too dry to eat, and the gum was like powder in his mouth, making it difficult even to spit out. A tin can in each ration contained stew, meat and beans, or cheese. The cheese was very good, but the others were not palatable when cold. Rex ate K-rations for a while, but he threw away most of the contents. After that, he drew rations only if the crew expected to be away more than one day.

One exceptionally dark morning, shortly after takeoff from Dum Dum, both engines on Rex's C-46 died. They had risen to only 1300 feet, so there was no time to buckle on a parachute, which Rex would have gladly used, had it already been strapped on. Instead, Rex made a silent promise to God: "If you'll get me back on the ground safely, I will never refuse to do anything you ask of me!"

The silence was the most frightful sound he had ever heard. Captain Hoos struggled to restart the engines. One coughed, sputtered to life, and ran shakily for a few minutes while the other gave a short series of bursts. Each engine seemed to take its cue from the other as they took turns sputtering, giving the plane just enough time and impulse to return safely to the airfield.

Rex was assigned the next flight out with another crew that was next in line to take off. When he returned, he was saddened to learn that Captain Hoos had died in a crash on takeoff that same day.[16] Most flights were without incident, and many were indeed a pleasure. Through the winter months, the skies were almost always clear, and occasionally there were views that would have been the envy of tourists. One time, they flew low over the Taj Mahal before landing. That afternoon, they were able to take a base bus and visit the fabulous tomb.

---

[16] While the bomber command crews were kept together throughout their term of duty, the ATC crewmembers, at least in the CBI theatre of operations, were all on separate lists. When each crewmember came in, his name went to the bottom of the list and worked its way to the top. With the shortage of radio operators, Rex's name came up before Captain Hoos' name, and thus they were not together on that tragic flight.

On one trip from New Delhi to Karachi, two giant mountain peaks rising above the horizon in the north caught Rex's attention. Looking at the charts, the pilot learned the mountains were two hundred miles away, but they were as visible as if they had been nearby. Another time in a C-46 with Captain Tom Cheatham at the controls, coming into the airfield at Agra, they flew over a fort similar to the feudal castles in Europe. Rex would have loved to visit the fort, but there was not enough time before they left the next morning.

They left Agra with almost the maximum load, 48,000 pounds gross. The landing gear was barely retracted when the left engine suddenly died. Had the gear not been up, the increased drag would certainly have caused a crash. After a long, straight, low flight, they gained sufficient altitude to turn around and Captain Cheatham brought the plane and crew safely back to Agra.

Despite his harrowing experiences, Rex liked the C-46. The thunder of the two thousand-horsepower engines seemed much more reassuring when the plane was being severely buffeted than did the quiet, efficient, 1350-horsepower engines on the C-47.

In Karachi, Rex met up again with Charley Poole, one of the men with whom he had spent many days waiting for an assignment while being shuttled from base to base in the States the year before. Charley and Rex jointly spent five rupees ($1.50) for a fighting cock and pitted it against the champion from the previous week.[17] They didn't know anything about fighting cocks, so they picked the one with brightest plumage. The person from whom they made the purchase fastened steel spurs to the feet of the cock and on the first exchange of blows, Charlie and Rex's bird spurred the opponent through the neck, and the fight was over. The *Hindustani Standard*, a local newspaper, reported the winners, giving Charlie and Rex the honor of having their names published throughout the Karachi area. When Rex again visited Karachi some weeks later, he learned their fame lasted only seven days, when their cock's demise came at the foot of some other bird.

Rex's favorite flight was to Columbo, Ceylon. Even though they often stayed only a few hours, the base at Columbo was in the most

---

[17] Cockfights were held weekly on the base in Karachi. Local residents brought fighting cocks to the field, sold them to the soldiers or airmen, then handled the birds and saved the survivors to fight the next week. While illegal in the US, this was common entertainment in that part of the world.

beautiful tropical setting imaginable. The headquarters sat under waving coconut palms. A soft sea breeze seemed to blow continuously. It was very peaceful, yet only a few hundred miles away raged the carnage of war.

Chapter 10

VJ DAY

When Burma had been freed from Japanese control, planes from Dum Dum flew the weary, and often sick, American troops over the mountains from Myitkyina, Burma to Calcutta, India. That was either the first leg of their journey back to the States or, more often than not, just the first leg of a journey to another base to prepare for the invasion of Japan.

On one such trip, loaded with soldiers, the superchargers on Rex's plane failed when they were at nearly the midpoint of the mountain range. With the lack of the added power, the ship was only able to maintain an altitude of ten thousand feet. As usual, the mountains were enveloped with clouds, and there was only a general knowledge of the location of the peaks that towered above the aircraft. Since the peaks were not as high toward Burma as they were if they headed on to Calcutta, they turned back. The passengers were not alerted to this problem and to say the soldiers were disappointed when they disembarked and found themselves where they'd started would be a gross understatement.

After the unneeded troops in Burma had been evacuated, the corpses of those who had perished were exhumed and flown to Calcutta. From there, their remains would be returned to their homes and families for burial. The planes used for this transport were used only for that purpose. The stench of decay never left the ship; the air in the plane returning to Burma was as foul as when it was filled with bodies.

The flight crews involved certainly grieved for those who had given their lives, but they also dreaded these flights. It was a disagreeable assignment, but every airman involved recognized that any of the corpses could well have been his own and willingly provided the service. It provided a small degree of comfort to family members waiting for the body of their son or husband.

On August 14, 1945, Rex was on a flight returning from Karachi when they landed at Gaya airfield in mid-afternoon. He would always remember that stopover because it was there he learned that Japan had surrendered earlier that day. There was a lot of "kick-back" celebration at the base. Throughout the war, beer had been tightly rationed, but that day there was no shortage of open cans at the airfield. When the plane was refueled, Rex waited longer than usual for the return of the pilot and co-pilot. They were joyous when they finally appeared and in no condition to complete the flight to Calcutta. He didn't relax the whole flight, but after what seemed an eternity, they landed safely back at their home base. It has been said that a C-47 would fly itself, and Rex was pleased that, apparently, that was the case.

Once Japan surrendered, most of the flights ended, and after several months of constant duty, Rex was pleased to have the privilege of attending chapel services again, as had been his custom prior to arriving at Dum Dum. After hearing only a few messages, Rex discovered that the chaplain really did not believe in Christ's miracles. He attempted to explain the New Testament miracles away as ordinary events that occurred because people followed Christ's example of compassion.

For some time, Rex struggled with the decision of whether to attend the chapel services. After considerable thought and prayer, he concluded it was better to attend. It was the only available gathering place for Christian services, and God commanded Christians to gather for worship. Rex believed that many others attended who shared his convictions.

Throughout the conflict, when an airman had flown a thousand hours, he was eligible for rotation. Rex had accumulated more than nine hundred hours in the air and believed he would be eligible to return to the States with a thousand hours now that the war was over. Flying emergency supplies to advance bases and delivering an increased volume of mail kept more planes in the air from Dum Dum than from other bases. Wanting the additional hundred hours, Rex volunteered for every flight available. This decision sped his return and enabled him to serve on two interesting missions.

Supplies that American forces no longer needed were given to the Chinese nationalists to help in their war against the communists. One such gift was a C-46 that was ferried to Shanghai. Rex was assigned to the crew. In those days, Shanghai was in a constant state of celebration, and silk goods were abundant. Rex bought two silk tablecloths and a couple of smaller items. Though silk was cheap, he only had the equivalent of fourteen U.S. dollars, so his purchase power was limited.

The most interesting flight was in October, when Rex was the radio operator on a crew sent to the Dutch East Indies (Indonesia) to survey the location of POWs and civilian internees. C-47 planes had a limited range without refueling, and the flight was to be almost entirely by visual contact with the ground. Because of these restrictions, overnight stops were made in Rangoon, Burma; Georgetown, Penang;[18] Bangkok, Thailand; and Singapore. The final destination was Batavia,[19] on the island of Java.

The crew could not leave anything of value in the plane or their rooms at the luxurious Hotel de Indies where they stayed. They ate in the hotel dining room, everyone but them was dressed in fine clothing, and Rex was embarrassed by the need to hitch the pistol from his hip so he could sit down. Weapons were out of place in such surroundings.

In spite of shortages, the food was well prepared, and the meals were a true dining pleasure. There was no flour for bread, but there was an abundance of delicious fruits and vegetables. A heavy, green Jell-O-like desert was also served. Rex never found out what it was, but it was especially tasty.

Though the C-47 was a twin-engine ship, an engineer was included for this assignment, as was a flight surgeon. The surgeon's assignment was to report on the condition of prisoners of war. He was the only member of the crew shown the POW camps, and he brought back disturbing reports. The concentration camp at Batavia was the worst of these dismal places. Residents had barely enough clothing to cover themselves and they were emaciated, similar to what European troops found in Nazi Germany the summer before.

From Batavia, the crew flew to different bases around the island, endeavoring to locate other prisoners. One such flight was to Malang in Eastern Java, the Japanese headquarters for the Southeast Asian Theater. The Japanese met Rex's plane with an honor guard and a band. Before the captain understood what was happening, the entire Southeast Asian Theater was formally surrendered to him. Even though he was the officer in charge, when the pilot learned what was being done, he was forced to decline. The Japanese had been instructed to maintain control until the Allies came, but surrender needed to be to troops who could maintain that control.

The people of the region, who had been under the heel of the Japanese for so many years, thought Americans could do no wrong. Residents on Penang, who wanted to see an American, surrounded the

---

[18] An island off the Malay Peninsula
[19] Now Jakarta

crew when they landed in Georgetown. In Java, the crew was idolized almost as much. When residents of the islands learned the British, not the Americans, would replace their Japanese captors, they were greatly disappointed.

The extra flights enabled Rex to complete a thousand hours of flight time in November. His elation turned to chagrin when he learned he was only one of a multitude waiting for transport home. Hundreds of thousands of troops were impatiently waiting to be sent home from all the theaters of war.

Most of the troops stationed in India and Burma boarded ships in Calcutta and returned home by sea. Planes ferried as many as possible. There were rumors that air travel could take longer than going by sea, but for those awaiting passage home any means of leaving India was desirable.

A system of priority had been established for those traveling by air. Top priority was given to the sick, injured, or disabled. The next priorities went to anyone who could arrange transportation. Because long-range airliners were many years in the future, traveling from Calcutta to the United States by air required stops at many airfields along the route. Any passenger could be removed for a higher priority passenger at any stopover.

On Dec. 28, 1945, Rex was suddenly told to clear the field. "You're on the crew of a C-54 going to the States," he was told. On the flight home, two crew chiefs, three radio operators, and nine pilots were assigned to the crew. The army air force cared for its own, and the operations officer knew no crewmember would be removed for priority.

The plane made overnight stops in Karachi, India; Abadan, Iran; Cairo, Egypt; Casablanca, Morocco; Accra, Gold Coast;[20] Ascension Island, and Natal, Brazil. Rex arrived at Morrison Field in West Palm Beach, Florida on January 5, 1946.

Some service personnel had been overseas continuously for four years. Rex had been away slightly less than a year. He was happy to have been able to serve his country, but he was glad to be back in the land he had grown to love even more than before the war.

Rex had expected to be discharged quickly, but he learned that after January 1, 1946, no one with less than two years service would be dis-

---

[20] Now Accra, Ghana

charged. He was given a twenty-day furlough and assigned to report to a base in Memphis, Tennessee. This was the start of the most emotionally difficult two years in the military. He did not understand the necessity of maintaining a sizable military force.[21] The war was over. Rex had served honorably, and there was no reason for him to be kept from his wife. He and Evelyn had been married only fifteen months when they were separated.

Rex had few useful duties. He cleaned buildings in camp, ran errands, and flew four hours a month just to keep his flight pay. All this time, he chafed internally. He was not able to control his resentment and became extremely bitter. Unfortunately, he clung to some of that bitterness after he was honorably discharged on May 6, 1946.

---

[21] The wisdom of that decision was made clear when the Korean War erupted.

Chapter 11

HOME AT LAST

Though Evelyn missed her husband while he was overseas, she was content working for her sister at the market in Pontiac, Michigan. She was well compensated and lived comfortably in Marian's home. Five nephews and nieces kept her from feeling alone.

Rex had already told her he did not plan to return to American Airlines when he was discharged, even though he was guaranteed reemployment. He seemed unsettled and unhappy. Evelyn could not understand why. It was not characteristic of the man she married.

Confident their marriage would continue in the same happy vein as in Chicago, Evelyn told Rex there was work for him in Pontiac and suggested they make their home there. Marian and Bill Lotan had said they would hire Rex upon his return home from the war. It was a means of keeping Evelyn on the payroll. Her marketing experience and constant smile were too valuable to let slip away.

Of course, Rex didn't know the reason for the offer, and if Evelyn knew, she certainly did not indicate it, but he didn't seriously consider the offer. He believed great opportunity awaited them on the farm, and he was determined to return to the home of his youth.

Harold was operating Grover and Grace's hundred and sixty-acre farm and had purchased another eighty acres nearby. Recently, he had learned that four hundred and eighty acres of newly logged land was available for three dollars an acre and suggested that he and Rex purchase it jointly. Harold was confident the previously forested land could soon become fertile, agricultural fields, even though it was still covered with large stumps. Rex saw only fields replacing the beautiful virgin forests he had loved as a youth, but that thought dimmed in light of the fact that he was coming home!

The great forest that had covered the property when Harold and Rex were young had been decimated, but the brothers were exuberant for the opportunity to own the land they had roamed as children. It was a bargain, and after borrowing the entire $1,440 from a neighbor, they proceeded with the purchase. Harold and Rex would have vehemently denied a subconscious desire to return to their happy childhood. In all probability, that yearning clouded their vision, but with more than a square mile of potentially fertile farmland, they felt their future was assured.

When Evelyn was convinced her husband would not be content in the city, she agreed to adjust her life to be with him. Rex had made no provision for housing, so Evelyn purchased a small travel trailer with money she had saved during Rex's absence and prepared to move to the farm. There would be no running water, and for the first time since her early childhood, Evelyn would need to use an outdoor toilet. There were other conveniences she would miss, but she believed being with her husband and having children would compensate for the hardships.

The 1936 Plymouth that Rex had purchased in the summer of 1941 had faithfully served him and Evelyn for five years. Now, with his wife beside him and the travel trailer in tow, Rex drove to the home where he had been born.

Grover had prepared a place under a beautiful maple tree for their son and his wife to park their little home. Grace prepared a feast the day of their arrival remembering Rex's favorite foods, including roast chicken, mashed potatoes and gravy, fresh homemade bread, and even pickles. Harold, Marie, and their little daughter Sherry shared in the welcome. Marie brought her famous chocolate fudge cake. It was a joyous homecoming for Rex, and if Evelyn had been reluctant to leave the comforts of city life, she did not betray her feelings.

Through a lifetime of hard work and persistence, Grover and Grace had developed the farm. The farm had been their life. When Grace's health prevented them from continuing, they invited Harold and Marie to take over and moved to the town of Kalkaska. Neither could bear the thought of selling it; it was their home. Grover loved Rock and Roxie, the team of Percheron draft horses he had raised from colts, but Harold would care for them well.

Grace loved working in the garden, though her health limited her activity. The garden had always been her place of respite in times of stress. The hymn, "In the Garden" expressed her sentiments. "I come to the garden alone, while the dew is still on the roses..." She often hummed the tune as she pulled weeds from the rows of vegetables.

Though Grover and Grace now lived ten miles away, they made the long trek and helped on the farm whenever they were able. They were pleased that the farm continued to operate, and it was a joy to see their life's work continuing through their children.

Though Harold and Rex made many plans for the future, they had never discussed and had apparently never considered the need for additional income to support a second family. The small herd of cattle provided dairy products for the three families and reasonable living expenses for one, but no more.

Though Rex had not planned well financially, God provided for the first of many unforeseen needs his family would encounter. The Veteran's Administration set up what came to be known as 52-20. All returning veterans were eligible to receive twenty dollars a week for a maximum of fifty-two weeks if needed. Rex seized on this temporary solution, but looked no further for another.

With the little money he had saved and some solicited from his wife's savings, Rex purchased a John Deere tractor. With a tractor, a good team of horses, and the additional farmland, Harold and Rex were confident the farm would soon support both families. Potatoes could be planted in the cleared fields of the newly purchased property. This would greatly supplement their income. The future was indeed promising.

Rex enjoyed the farm work. Life with Evelyn was even better than he remembered. Her constant smile and warm welcome when he returned from the fields was a sharp contrast to the idleness and regimentation he had endured while awaiting discharge.

Rex sang as he rode the tractor throughout the day. Harold loved working with Rock and Roxie, and Rex was happy to let him. Rex had never been very good with horses. Harold pulled stumps in preparation for the next year's crops while Rex prepared the existing fields and did the planting.

One especially beautiful evening in July, Evelyn took Rex's hand, smiled wistfully, and said, "Rex, I'm twenty-seven years old. If we are going to have children, we should start having them soon." The thought of parenthood was foreign to Rex, but the expression on Evelyn's face spoke far more eloquently than her words. Evelyn waited briefly before continuing, "You'll love a baby as much as I will."

If Evelyn wanted a child, Rex wanted one also, even if it were just to please her. Rex smiled as he hugged his lovely wife. "I don't think I could be any happier than I am now," he said. "I loved Mary and Glenn's children. I'll love ours even more."

In time, Evelyn became more content. In spite of feeling nauseous most mornings throughout the summer and autumn, her constant smile brightened their little home. One day, awaking to the limitations of their eight-by-sixteen-foot trailer, Rex said, "We can't live here with a family. I'll have to build a house."

Directly across the section road from Grover and Grace, on a part of the newly purchased acreage, was a small hill, which Evelyn and Rex chose for their home. They cleared a small area and had a well drilled. With a gasoline engine to pump the water, Rex worked each evening on the basement. When it was completed, he said, "Next year, I'll build the house."

One night, they were awakened by a strong thunderstorm. Rex shared with Evelyn the story of that dark morning in India when the plane engines failed shortly after takeoff. The darkness, the deathly still-ness, and the realization there wasn't time to don his parachute was vivid in Rex's memory. He was convinced God had intervened to bring the ship back to the base safely. Though Evelyn listened carefully, there was no way Rex could communicate what he experienced on that flight.

The fury of the storm kept them both awake, and they spent some time reminiscing about the many good things in their lives that they believed could not have come about by accident. Rex told Evelyn about the lack of Bible teaching he had received in the chapel services and said he didn't think the church they were now attending was much bet-ter. Evelyn agreed. All too soon, the morning sun shone brightly on the fields and on Evelyn and Rex's hearts. The storm seemed to have brought them closer. They decided to visit a country church a few miles south of them, where Charles Opitz was ministering. Only a few fami-lies attended, but the enthusiasm of the young minister was contagious.

Pastor Opitz taught that salvation came only through faith in Jesus Christ and regularly pointed out the many references in the Bible that supported his teaching. Evelyn and Rex felt at home there and attended regularly. They loved the pastor greatly and were happy that their small tithe would help support him.

In October, when the corncrib was full and the winter supply of hay was in the barn, Harold and Rex shouldered their shotguns and hunted partridge[22], reminiscing about their childhood.

Harold could hardly wait to introduce his brother to the excitement of hunting deer. Deer often hid in the cedar swamp in the little valley

---

[22] Roughed grouse or ruffed grouse; many in northern Michigan commonly called them partridge, or even "pats" for short

along Rapid River. When the season opened in November, Harold was confident they would find deer there. He set Rex in a narrow strip of woods where deer often ran out and then circled back, walking through the thick cedars in the swamp toward Rex's position. The deer appeared where Harold had expected, and Rex killed his first buck. Deer hunting was exciting, and venison was delicious. It would be several years before Rex killed another deer, but November 15, simply called "opening day" in Michigan, became a holiday every year from then on.

Throughout the winter, the brothers cut firewood to sell and to warm their own homes. They needed additional income, but were often distracted by the abundance of snowshoe rabbits.[23] Harold and Rex took their shotguns to the woods with them, just in case. When their dog Pepper barked on a rabbit track, the temptation to lay down their saws and pick up their guns was greater than they could resist. Each time, they thought they would quickly kill the rabbit and resume wood-cutting, but all too often, hunting consumed the balance of the day.

---

[23] Technically, snowshoe hares

Chapter 12

REALITY

W hen the daylight hours lengthened in March and signaled a new beginning for fauna of all kinds, Harold and Rex began planning their summer. The excitement of hunting the previous autumn became a dim memory as they embraced the planting season.

A four-acre field of potatoes had been very profitable the year before. A seven-acre field had been prepared this year on Harold's eighty-acre parcel. He and Rex planned to increase their potato acreage as much each year as possible. The four hundred and eighty acres they had purchased had great long-term potential, but it was full of stumps that needed to be rooted out. They needed more land now to plant to corn and hay to provide for a larger dairy herd.

Grace's cousin, Fred Williams, owned eighty acres adjacent to Grover and Harold's property, sixty acres of which was idle farmland. Maybe that could provide an answer to their dilemma. Rex and Evelyn drove to Fred and Florence's home in Elk Rapids and told them of their need for farmland the coming summer.

At first, neither Fred nor Florence was interested in selling, but seeing the disappointment on Rex's face, Fred said. "We'll never do anything with that land. They might as well use it." For six hundred dollars, Rex and Evelyn purchase eighty acres of their own. When this was added to the four hundred and eighty acres of stumps and brush, Grover's hundred and sixty, and Harold's eighty, the Southwell brothers' farm and holdings became a sizable operation. Rex was pleased to have as much individually owned land as his brother. The future looked rosy indeed.

Shortly after midnight in the early morning of May 10, 1947, Evelyn shook her soundly sleeping husband. "I think our baby will be born today," she said. Evelyn really wanted her husband awake with her as she counted the minutes between the pains that warned of the coming birth.

At two a.m., Rex and Evelyn decided it was time to go and hurried to Munson Hospital in Traverse City, but the child was in no hurry. Evelyn struggled for hours, most of them in the delivery room. Hour after hour, Rex waited for word, but none came. Eventually, a man came from the delivery room with an empty oxygen tank, disappeared into the elevator, then returned to the delivery room with a replacement. Still, there was no word.

Rex was sure he would soon be alone in this world. His mother had told him and his brothers of the dangers of giving birth. Their neighbor, Anna Nichols, had died in childbirth. Rex's imagination ran wild. Evelyn was surely dying, if she wasn't already dead. Why didn't someone tell him?

Finally, after twelve long hours, a lady emerged from the delivery room and presented Rex with a beautiful baby. Rex hardly looked at the newborn. "What about my wife?"

"Oh, she's fine," the nurse answered, apparently surprised at the question. Only then did Rex really turn his attention to his first child, a baby daughter.

After another seemingly interminable time, Rex was finally allowed to enter the delivery room, where a very tired, but happy Evelyn took his hand and feebly said, "She's a nice baby." They had long ago chosen the name Kay if their baby was a daughter. Their friends in Chicago, Jack and Rose Reiff, had a lovely little girl by that name. Kay's middle name would be Ellen. It was as near Evelyn as her mother would allow.

The eight-by-sixteen-foot trailer had been comfortable for Rex and Evelyn, but for a family of three, it was not adequate. Rex hoped to be able to build the shell of their house after the crops were harvested, then finish the inside during the winter months.

"There are a lot of good logs left in the felled treetops on the land you bought," Grover said. "They'll give you lumber for your house if you can get them sawed." Rex purchased an old, but usable, sawmill. It took half the money Evelyn had saved, but he was sure the mill would save them much more than it cost them.

In early summer, the twenty-dollar weekly income ceased. The income from the milk checks was then divided between the two families. Finances were extremely tight, and both brothers decided another source of income would have to be found until a few more heifers blossomed into milking cows.

Fortunately, God indirectly supplied an income that would meet the needs of Rex's family. The federal government set up an educational program for farm youths returning from service, similar to what was provided for those who wished to attend college. In each community, provisions could be made to establish an agricultural class for returning veterans. Farm youths would then receive the same subsistence payment given those attending college classes.

The agricultural agents and local business people saw this as not only a great help for returning farm youths, but also a financial boost for the community. After they found a local farmer who had graduated from an agricultural college and was a qualified instructor, the program was established in Kalkaska County. The subsistence payment would provide for Rex and his family for three years. Surely, by the end of three years, the farm would easily be able to provide for his family as well as his brother's family. Once again, Rex and Evelyn marveled at the provision of their Lord and joined in thanksgiving with exultation.

Twenty acres along the east side of Harold's eighty acres had not been farmed for many years, and many small trees had grown up. They hired a neighbor to bulldoze the trees, and Harold, with the help of Rock and Roxie, prepared ten of those acres for the next year's potato crop. Whenever they had an opportunity, Rex and Harold cut logs from the best of what Antrim Iron Company had left in the woods and cut them into lumber for Rex and Evelyn's house. When they finally began cutting the corn and digging the potatoes, the two brothers looked back with satisfaction upon a summer of great accomplishment.

Chapter 13

ACCIDENT

S now blanketed the farm and woodlands in early November 1947. Pepper was barking on a rabbit track incessantly and the urge to follow him was almost more than Rex and his brother could resist, but a lot of corn shocks still remained in the fields.

Harold had purchased a corn shredder, which was a marvelous time saver. Corn stalks were fed through the live rollers. , which snapped off the ears of corn, removed the husks, and shredded the stalks. Much of the fodder (shredded stalks and leaves) was then fed to the cattle. What was not eaten was used as straw to bed down the livestock. Remembering the long winter hours they spent in the haymow husking corn in their youth, Harold and Rex appreciated a machine to relieve them of that burden.

The weather was far too cold to work with bare hands, and one morning, as Harold fed the stalks of corn into the shredder, his glove caught and his hand was pulled into the rolls. As he fell against the safety bar, the rolls stopped, but his hand was stuck fast. Rex stopped the machine and slowly turned the pulley backward until his brother's hand was free, but it was immediately evident that the fingers and hand were crushed to the middle of the palm.

Rex and Harold's wife Marie rushed him to Dr. Rogers in Bellaire. The doctor gave first aid, called Munson Hospital in Traverse City, and sent them on to the emergency room. From ten a.m. until late afternoon, Marie and Rex waited impatiently for news from the operating room, but none ever came. Around four p.m. someone came from the information desk to inquire why they were there. It was only then that Harold finally received medical attention. When Marie and Rex eventually saw the doctor, they learned how serious the injury really was. Harold needed to stay in the hospital, and since there was no insurance, the hospital bill would have to be paid in advance. Rex had to bring money each day for the next day's care, so he sold one of their dairy cows each day to pay the bill. When Harold was released from the hospital, the dairy herd had been reduced to two cows. These would supply the families with milk and butter, but there was nothing left over to sell.

After three days, Dr. Powers told Harold the fingers would have to be amputated. The injury had destroyed the blood vessels, and the fingers were no longer alive. Harold's right hand now consisted of a thumb and a short stump for a first finger. The other fingers were gone.

The hospital bill had been paid, but there was no money to pay the doctor. Harold and Rex dreaded the expected bill. When Dr. Powers released Harold, he said there would be no bill for his services. Harold had lost enough.

Rex always believed that if Harold had received prompt medical attention in the emergency room, the fingers could have been saved, and he suspected that Dr. Powers believed it also, so felt constrained to donate his services.

Harold, Marie, and their two children now had no income. Harold could not work the farm or cut wood, so Rex and Evelyn divided their subsistence payment with them. Life was austere, but they were determined to survive until the cattle herd was replaced.

Farm work and then the accident had taken precedence over building a house for Evelyn. Through the summer, logs had been cut and lumber milled, but there had been little time for construction. Grover and Rex struggled through December to get the house enclosed before really bad weather set in. If they could get the roof on, they could work inside during the winter and finish the house sufficiently to move in. Their efforts fell short, however. When the first big snowstorm came, the walls were up, but not the roof.

It was a difficult winter for Evelyn. It was hard to care for Kay in their cramped quarters. Water had to be carried from Grover and Grace's well, and the only toilet facilities were an outhouse. Every time anyone came in, they tracked mud and snow all over the trailer.

Rex's workload increased greatly during Harold's recovery, but his wife and daughter greeted him every night with warm smiles. Their love sustained him through the winter. In March, Evelyn placed Kay on Rex's lap and told him Kay was to have a sibling. The pregnancy came as a surprise, but the young couple was pleased. Their second child had come a bit sooner than they would have chosen, but they did want more children. Now they really needed their new house before the following winter. Evelyn couldn't possibly care for two children in the trailer. That night, overwhelmed by the events of the year, they spent their Bible reading and prayer time thanking God for their little home and for providing for their needs.

Harold adapted to the limited use of his right hand. In the spring of 1948, he and Rex planted clover in the fields where the previous year's potato and corn crops had been, but they were not able to pull stumps to prepare additional cropland. An area was cleared and fenced for a sheep pasture. The sheep ate the small brush and sprouts, killing the vegetation, and enabling the struggling farmers to clear farmland more quickly.

A small addition to the barn was made. Even though most of the milking cattle had been sold, more room was needed for young cattle and the small flock of sheep they had purchased. Summer on the farm was a pleasure. The work was hard and the hours long, but the abundant vegetables, the yearling steers, and the young pigs butchered in November provided excellent table fare throughout the year.

Rex and Evelyn became more active in their church, and in early summer, they were asked to hold weekly meetings for the young people of the area. They were convinced this request was from God and agreed to help. Though neither of them was well versed in the scriptures or had ever led a church group of any kind, they began meeting with a small group on Wednesday evenings at the church. Evelyn and Rex picked up young people near their home until they could not pack another person in the car. Soon ten or fifteen teenagers were meeting weekly.

There were no competing activities, and the youths were glad to get together. A few old hymnbooks were available, and the group enthusiastically sang the few songs they knew, even without musical accompaniment. Each week, Rex read a passage from the Bible and commented on it to the best of his ability.

Rex and Evelyn weren't sure if the young people found the lessons interesting or just enjoyed the companionship, but three of the group accepted Christ as their savior and many years later expressed appreciation for the Bible lessons. Later on, when more youths were attending from nearby than from the church area, they moved the meetings to their home. Happy and focused on his limited ministry for God, Rex shut his eyes to the financial reality that would soon face him and his family.

Grover and Grace looked on their sons' situation with sorrow. They saw the handwriting on the wall. Farm production was not enough to provide for both families when the VA payments ended. Their sons had made no progress in transforming the four hundred and eighty acres of stumps into farmland, and any effort Grover or Grace made to awaken their sons to impending doom was sharply rebuffed. Their sons seemed either unable to understand or to not care.

Grover worked harder than Rex did to make the new house habitable. They had no time to complete the second story and \ roof before Evelyn gave birth to their second child, so Grover suggested they put a flat roof on what they had built and prepare for winter. On Labor Day 1948, Rex, Evelyn, and Kay moved into their new home.

By the standards of that day, it was roomy. There was a large kitchen, dining room, living room, and bedroom. A small sun parlor graced the west side, while a bathroom and closet separated the bedroom from the living room. A sink and cold-water faucet was ready for use in the kitchen. Though there were still no bathroom facilities, Grover had provided a rough outdoor toilet. Rex promised to have bathroom fixtures in before winter.

Evelyn was grateful for the increased comfort. The next child would be coming soon, and there was no room in the little trailer for a family of four. The promised bathroom would make caring for the babies much easier. She now had a roomy kitchen, but for the first time in her life, she had to cook on a wood range. That mattered little because she now had a larger cooking surface, and finally, an oven.

Autumn in northern Michigan is beautiful. The maple leaves were especially brilliant that year. Their golden splendor was interspersed with yellow and brown from other trees. A few green leaves still struggled to maintain their color. Brilliant red sumac dominated some areas. A peaceful, rural life was the reward for the physical struggle and uncertainty of the farm.

Chapter 14

A SON AND GRANDSON

D avid Bryce Southwell came into the world mid-afternoon, September 28, 1948, at Munson Hospital in Traverse City, where Kay had been born sixteen months previously. His birth brought much less pain to his mother and much less anxiety to his father than his sister's had.

Grover was pleased. David was their fourth grandchild, but their first grandson, and he could carry on the family name. Rex was helping Kay with her supper that evening when Grover quietly said, "The bathroom needs to be finished before Evelyn comes home." He spoke softly, as though thinking aloud, but his voice was firm.

Rex agreed. "Yes, it has to be finished," he thought. "Dad's done most of the work on the bathroom already, but I'll have to help."

Ruefully, Rex realized that Grover's determination to finish the house had been far greater than his own. Without Grover, there would have been no house. Without Grover, Evelyn would have no bathroom. They worked well into the night the evening before Evelyn and David came home, and Rex became concerned for his father. Grover's body, which had served him well for almost sixty years, was frail. The determination he had developed through a lifetime of work enabled him to finish the job, but the late night work was tough, and Grover tired far more easily than in the past.

The following afternoon, Grover and Grace impatiently awaited Rex's return with their grandson. Children had always held a priority in their lives, and they dearly loved their grandchildren. Grover was also eager for Evelyn to see the bathroom. It was a luxury he had not yet been able to provide for his own wife, but it would be a great help for his daughter-in-law, who had two young children to care for.

Evelyn, David, and Rex returned at suppertime, and Grace had a meal in the warming oven for all of them. Grace held their first grandson while Kay looked wonderingly into the little baby's face. Evelyn watched proudly. After a short time, Rex plucked David from his mother's hands and beckoned for Evelyn to follow him to the bathroom, where he walked to the sink and turned on a faucet. Evelyn gasped and then moved over and flushed the toilet. Tears filled her eyes as she hugged her husband.

Rex gently turned her face toward his father and said simply, "Thank him." Rex's eyes watered also. Evelyn's happiness and his appreciation for everything his father and mother had done for them overwhelmed him. For Grover, Evelyn's pleasure was his reward. He could now relax. It had been a struggle, but Rex and Evelyn were comfortably into their own house. Rex had to shoulder the responsibility for the remaining work.

By late October, the kitchen range no longer provided sufficient heat for the new house. Rex found a cheap sheet metal stove, similar to what was used in the logging camps years earlier, and installed it. It wasn't the best option, but was all he could afford.

One cold November evening, Rex came in from milking the cows and sat down on the couch with his children. He and Evelyn thanked God for their house. It was unfinished, inside and out, but they were warm, and there was plenty of room for the two children. As the snow beat against the windows and the wind whipped the trees, Evelyn said, "I'm sure thankful for the bathroom."

The little sheet metal stove was heated to a dull red, but the house was warm. Evelyn stood with her back to the stove watching Rex with the children and enjoying the radiant heat.

Suddenly, she screamed, "My dress is on fire!"

Rex grabbed the back of the dress, tore most of it off, and patted the remaining flames out with his hands. They hadn't realized the stove could ignite Evelyn's dress, but obviously, the open draft on the front was a hazard. They would have to watch the children carefully. There were severe blisters on Evelyn's legs, but a greater disaster had been averted. Once again, God had watched over their little family.

Grace prepared for Thanksgiving dinner and invited her sons' families to share the special holiday with them. The big barred rock rooster that attacked anyone who passed his way was roasted for the occasion. Hubbard squash, mashed potatoes, pickles, and Grace's traditional steamed carrot pudding were more than sufficient to fill everyone's stomach. That afternoon, Rex and Harold got out the Monopoly game. In their youth, they had occupied many a wintry Sunday afternoon circling the game board, buying and selling properties, and collecting rent from the other players. Now it was exciting to play the game with their parents and spouses.

After Thanksgiving, Rex and Harold began cutting stove wood in earnest. Extra income was a necessity, and all three homes required fuel for the winter. Occasionally, they wondered aloud how they could expand the dairy herd to gain a more regular income. Calves were becoming cows, but the process was slow. Besides, they still needed a new barn. There never seemed to be a satisfactory answer to how to proceed. Which should they do first with their meager funds, buy more dairy cows or build a barn to hold them? They could not do both. When Grover and Grace were consulted, they painted a dismal picture for the two brothers—one their sons were unwilling to see and accept. Grover was blunt. "You'll soon be broke."

Harold and Rex both remembered their childhood. Their parents had plodded along. One section of the barn was added at a time. When there was enough hay and grain, they added another cow, but neither Rex nor Harold was willing to take the slow route. Large farms were doing well, but Harold and Rex needed more fields, more livestock, and a much bigger barn.

Rex asked advice from some of the more affluent farmers and businessmen. All had suggestions, but none was financially possible for them. Rex and Harold lacked cash. The instructions in the agricultural class stressed sound agricultural practice, which presumably enhanced crop production, but financial considerations were not part of the course.

Orville Walker, the county agricultural agent, had been successful with an expensive soil enrichment program called the Walker Quickie. Mr. Walker had received considerable notoriety throughout the state and was pushing the plan fervently. Many questioned whether the high costs could be recovered, but Mr. Walker was optimistic. Rex and Harold bought into his optimism and blindly followed every new program the county agent recommended.

Most VA payments to veterans quickly found their way into the pockets of those providing supplies to the young farmers. Business was booming for dealers in farm equipment and supplies. They were extending credit beyond what was wise, and Harold and Rex were a part of the many going deeply into debt. Apparently, few if any businesses looked beyond the end of the VA program upon which this instant prosperity was founded. If they had, they had decided to milk the program to its fullest while it was available.

New associations were being formed, and in the winter months, Rex was elected to the board of directors of the Dairy Herd Improvement Association, the Red Dane (cattle) Association, and the Soil

Conservation District. In retrospect, Rex honestly never knew if he accepted those positions because he thought he was obediently following his promise to "never refuse to do anything God asked," or if it was foolish pride. He had never been a leader, and it was gratifying to be elected time after time. Many years later, Rex remembered the ease with which one could be elected to non-paying positions.

Rex and Evelyn received a devastating blow one Sunday morning during the church service. Pastor Opitz was leaving to minister a church in Iowa. They loved their pastor and his family dearly, and they had learned much from his teaching, but the pastor explained that there was insufficient income from the church to care for his family's physical needs.

The church been closed through the troubled years of 1941-45. When it reopened, those who attended were far from affluent. They had contributed in concert with their ability to give, but the small group was never able to meet even the pastor and his family's basic needs. After three years of financial hardship, the pastor could no longer serve them.

Rex and Evelyn began attending the services of a young missionary couple, Willard and Millie Bontrager, who had started a church in a nearby schoolhouse. Gradually, Rex and Evelyn realized that even though Willard taught salvation through faith in Christ, there were church policies with which they could not agree. They needed to find a different church in which to raise their children.

In spite of the financial situation, some progress was being made on the farm. More acres were planted to corn in the summer of 1949. Some old fencerows were cleared, troublesome stumps were blown out with dynamite, and more than two miles of new fence was strung. However, there they had still not been able to make significant additions to their dairy herd and they had not been able to develop any of the four hundred and eighty acres they had purchased into farmland.

Neither Harold nor Rex saw the financial crisis that was looming ever nearer. Even when Grover attempted to acquaint Rex with the pitfalls they were facing, Rex refused to listen. Rex thought his father did not understand the changes taking place in agriculture. Heavy snowfall in the winter of 1949-50 kept Harold and Rex from cutting wood to sell as they had done in prior years. When they could no longer provide for even the basic needs of their families, the financial squeeze they were in finally became apparent to them.

Rex sought more advice from the prosperous farmers when he attended the board of directors meetings of the various farm organizations. In one session, Rex asked if it would be wise for him and his brother to give up farming. The one remaining year of veteran benefits was not going to enable them to become self-supporting. He thought they should sell the machinery and livestock, and pay their creditors, but the county agricultural agent didn't want anyone to fail, and the dealers who sold most of the products on credit did not seem worried.

Chapter 15

ANOTHER EFFORT

Orville Walker, the Kalkaska County agricultural agent, suggested to Rex and Harold that they raise foundation certified seed potatoes.[24] Such a crop might be the answer to their need to boost their income, since foundation seed potatoes sold for far more than regular certified seed. In addition, Mr. Walker thought the Southwell brothers could still be successful if they introduced a new variety of potatoes and used his soil enrichment program to ensure maximum production.

Rex was eager to follow Mr. Walker's advice and Harold made no objection. They had followed the recommendations of the agriculture instructor and the county agricultural agent this far and the proposed plan might bring them the success they desired. Rex had attained considerable status in the community, and he enjoyed hobnobbing with community leaders. Pride would not let him consider the risk of planting the proposed crop or entertain thoughts of failure.

In the spring of 1950, even though Rex's subsistence payments had ceased, he and Harold followed Mr. Walker's suggestion and applied his notorious "Walker Quickie" soil enrichment program to an eleven-acre field. Local businesses were more than eager to provide the necessary credit if Harold and Rex followed Mr. Walker's advice. In June, the field was planted to buckwheat with four hundred pounds of 12-12-12 fertilizer[25] per acre in preparation for the following year's crop. Buckwheat matures quickly, and in late August, the land was a mass of green reaching above the knees.

---

[24] There was so much disease in potatoes that many growers never saved seed potatoes from their own crop for the following year's planting. Instead they purchased certified seed potatoes that were examined throughout the year by the state department of agriculture and "certified" as acceptably free from disease. In turn, growers of certified seed were required to plant "foundation certified" seed. Again, the State Department of Agriculture certified the quality of foundation certified seed, but virtually no deviation from perfection was allowed. Growers of foundation certified seed could plant their own seed year after year unless something disqualified their crop.
[25] The numbers that label fertilizer represent amounts nitrogen, phosphoric acid, and potash, respectively.

On August 20, Rex and Harold plowed under the buckwheat and planted rye with another four hundred pounds of fertilizer. The rye grew quickly and was a lush green when the first snow fell in November. Few other farm crops had been planted that year other than the "Walker Quickie." With no other income, Harold and Rex cut and sold pulpwood in the summer and stove wood in the winter to provide food for their families.

Rex and Evelyn lived an austere life. Evelyn was frugal and could feed and clothe the family with the meager income. She trusted her husband for a more comfortable future, but she could not help but notice the appearance of their home. She was grateful for the bathroom, but few other improvements had been made. Cheap building paper covered the inside walls and the exterior of the house was still protected only by fading tarpaper.

Occasionally Evelyn considered how different their lives would have been if they had stayed in Pontiac or if Rex had returned to American Airlines, but she never complained. She knew Rex loved her and the children. He was doing what he could for the family, and she was confident conditions would improve over time. Those thoughts let her enjoy her two young children in spite of the difficulties.

In the spring of 1951, the rye came up a dark green matt. When it was plowed under in mid-May, the soil did indeed appear well infused with organic matter. The two brothers purchased Foundation Sebago seed potatoes with a loan from the bank and planted them with another six hundred pounds of fertilizer per acre. It would take a great crop and a good price to keep Rex and Harold in farming, but they were optimistic.

On May 26, 1951, Evelyn gave birth to Donald Gene Southwell at Meadowbrook Hospital in Bellaire. Rex wanted the middle name to be Jean, after his close friend Jean Cunningham, but following Jean's recommendation and Evelyn's insistence, they spelled his middle name Gene. Jean Cunningham frequently received mail or messages to Miss Jean Cunningham, and he was sure Don would be happier with the other spelling.

By mid-July, the potato field was in full bloom, and vines completely covered the ground. Though the "Walker Quickie" had been extremely expensive, it appeared worth the cost. Harold and Rex walked admiringly through the field, confident of an abundant harvest. Before long, they would learn if their five years on the farm would be rewarded with success or if their efforts had been in vain. Rex wondered aloud if they should have applied a Walker Quickie to a second field that summer, but Harold remarked ruefully that no one would advance them that much more credit. Neither recognized they had made no plans for future years.

In mid-August, a devastating frost covered the entire area, and the potato vines were killed a full month before maturity. There had been frosts in mid-summer many years earlier, but no one expected it would happen again. In one night, their crop yield was reduced from a projected four to five hundred bushels per acre to only a hundred and fifty bushels of very small potatoes per acre. Their last hope for farming success had been dashed.

Selling their crop shouldn't be a problem because the small potatoes, referred to as "size B," were preferred for planting. They produced as bountifully as the cut pieces of larger potatoes and were much easier to plant. Also, even though the potatoes were small, the price per bushel could be very high. Foundation certified seed potatoes should sell for five dollars or more per bushel. Though they would have no profit, maybe they could at least pay their creditors.

One could argue that Harold and Rex had planned well during their first years, but when Harold's injury forced them sell the livestock, it crippled them, and they failed to make proper adjustments. Each evening, a defeated Rex came home to his wife and children, but he was always greeted by a bright smile from Evelyn and joyous hugs from Kay and David. Little Don slept peacefully in his crib. Life had taken a bad turn for them, but it would go on.

The potatoes were dug and carefully stored in Evelyn and Rex's basement. They were practically worthless until the following spring so it was necessary to isolate them from other potatoes to protect them from disease. Throughout the winter, the potatoes kept very well, but for Evelyn and their family, all was not well. The humidity kept the windows steamed all through the cold weather and the odor of potatoes pervaded the house.

In February, Evelyn again became pregnant. The economic picture was dismal, but they were pleased at the thought of another child. God had provided before and he would provide for this child also. The few cattle the Southwells still owned provided dairy products for both brothers' families and their parents. There was feed in the barn for the animals, but once again, there was no farm income.

Grover and Grace had previously worked in Grand Rapids and suggested Harold go to the city and work with them that winter. He accepted the suggestion and found a job in the railroad yard with his father. He shared his check with Rex and Evelyn. Because Evelyn was pregnant and had three small children, Rex could not leave his family, but there was plenty of work to do. Two hundred small logs remained in the woods. Harold and Rex had cut them to sell as cross ties to the Pennsylvania Railroad, but when they failed to deliver them in the allotted time, the contract had been canceled. Rex skidded the logs, cut firewood from the treetops for both families, milked the cows morning and night, and cared for the livestock.

In spite of Rex's reluctance to work with horses, Rock and Roxie held no grudge against him. In a short time, their willingness and cooperation with their green teamster had its effect. It was difficult to bring the team in, wipe the snow off their backs, put hay in the manger, and see them expectantly look for grain without giving them a friendly pat and a few more oats. Grover's prize Percheron colts were now about fifteen years old. They were still his pride and joy and were now working their way into Rex's heart.

In early May 1952, Mr. Walker brought a customer for the potatoes. Harold quit his job in Grand Rapids and the brothers graded and carried their crop out of the basement. It had been a hard to get them into the basement, but carrying the hundred-pound bags up the stairway was even more difficult. The potatoes had kept very well, and it seemed the income would indeed pay their debts.

The potato inspector carefully surveyed the brothers' diminished crop. A final blow came when he found a potato with ring-rot. This was a dreaded disease for which there was no tolerance in certified seed. That one bad potato disqualified the entire crop, not only as foundation seed but also as regular certified seed. Mr. Walker did what he could. He found a potato grower who purchased them as regular seed potatoes. They received only a dollar-fifty per bushel, not the five or six dollars they had hoped for certified seed.

The brothers paid their small creditors. The two farm stores were given a token payment, and the balance was paid to the bank. Huge debts remained. A totally defeated Rex faced his wife without a plan. Even then, Evelyn continued to smile. What was behind the smile only Evelyn knew, but her husband needed her now more than ever before.

She displayed great faith and trust, because their fourth child was due in October—just five months off.

Esther Dunlap, a former Sunday school teacher, neighbor, and close friend, sympathetically said to Rex, "When God slaps you down he slaps you down hard, doesn't he?"

Esther was right. Rex knew he had been too proud to take advice from those who loved him. The excitement of serving with area leaders and undue optimism had blinded him to reality. While other veterans used their GI bill money to obtain an education, he had invested his in a losing effort.

Rex had left military service determined to take orders from no one. For six years, he had taken neither orders nor advice, and now he was paying a heavy price for that freedom. Harold had been a willing partner, but Rex felt responsible for their failure.

Grover and Grace were saddened that the farm for which they had given their lives could not be continued, but their love for their children would not allow them to condemn them for this financial tragedy. Somehow, in some way, Rex would find a way to care for the family God had given him.

Evelyn at 18 months

Evelyn at Torch Lake 1937

Rex at sales office Lake City 1939

Harold Jean Rex from left to right 1940

Rex woking at gas station 1941

Rex & Evelyn Wedding Day Jan 17 1943

Rex & Evelyn Wedding Picture 1943

Rex WW 2 1945

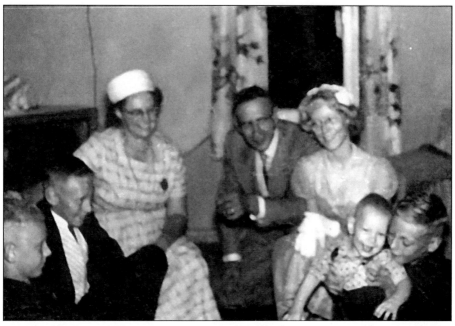

Rex, Evelyn and Family 1960

Rex and Evelyn's Home 1975

Evelyn with daughter Kay 1991

Rex, Evelyn and Family at 50th Anniversary

Rex and Evelyn's 59 Anniversary

Rex by Southwell Lake 2008

Rex enjoying retirement 2008

Rex overlooking Southwell Lake 2008

Chapter 16

FRESH START

H arold and Rex grimly considered their financial obligations. It was not a pretty picture. Six years of business failure had cost them dearly, but neither blamed the other. Their joint obligations totaled over seven thousand dollars. They still had four hundred and eighty acres of wild land and property values were rapidly increasing. While the sale of all or part of that holding might have held a solution for their immediate finances, each hill and valley brought memories of their happy childhood, and they were obsessed by the desire to hold on to that cherished property.

The payments they had already made on their debts would hopefully buy them some time with their creditors, but that left no income for personal expenses. They were on the verge of being destitute. The brothers discussed this and thought if their families could be supported with outside income, continuing to operate the farm might eventually pay their debts.

They agreed each would be responsible for his own family. They would no longer share income, other than that generated by the farm. All farm income would be divided among their creditors, and each would contribute as much as possible to keep the farm operating.

Harold found work at Mt. Clemens Metal Products, a small automobile parts manufacturing plant in Mancelona. Rex made other plans. American Excelsior Company was buying peeled softwood bolts. The bolts were cut from either poplar or basswood trees, debarked, cut into 55-inch lengths, loaded onto a boxcar, and shipped. The purchasing company then shredded them for packaging material. Rex obtained an order from the American Excelsior Company for a train carload of bolts and immediately set himself to the arduous task of cutting, debarking, and loading a carload of twenty-two cords.

The income was good, but Rex had greater ambitions. He believed by hiring three men, he could cut and ship a carload a week. With a net income of a hundred dollars per load, his income would nearly double what men in the local factory were being paid.

There was an abundance of state-owned property from which Rex could purchase timber, and by early September, the goal of shipping a carload a week was realized. Rex enjoyed working in the timber. Even though it was hard work, it gave him a sense of accomplishment, so he began to plan for greater things.

Evelyn never complained about the deprivation under which they had been living. She was grateful for each dollar Rex earned and brought home. Rex and Harold worked evenings on the farm. The two cows they still owned furnished milk and butter for the families. The calves were growing and would be sold in the autumn to make another payment on the debt. Their creditors had agreed to be patient. Last year's corn and potato fields were seeded to clover, but no new crops were planted because neither brother could find time to work the fields.

In late September, Rex received a call from American Excelsior. They didn't want any more bolts. "We ordered one carload from you," they said, "and we've received three." Rex was devastated. Not only were his dreams shattered, there were two more carloads on the way to Grand Rapids. The company agreed to accept the two carloads of bolts, but there would be no additional orders.

Evelyn and Rex prayed diligently for wisdom as to what they should do for income. Checks from the two remaining carloads of bolts would tide them over for only a short while. At least food was not a problem. The garden provided them with produce, and the cows provided them with an abundance of milk and butter. Meat, however, was in a very limited supply. Rex used the down time to cut and pile wood for the winter. The chain saw he had purchased for cutting bolts made the job quicker and easier.

In October, God opened the windows of heaven and poured special blessings down on the struggling family. First, they received an invitation to attend a small Baptist church that had begun holding services in Kalkaska two years earlier. Evelyn and Rex had never attended a Baptist church before. Their first Sunday, they were greeted warmly. The pastor's sermons were delivered with fervor at least equal to Pastor Opitz. The pastor and his wife had great musical ability, which made that part of the service superb. Evelyn and Rex agreed to attend, at least for a while.

The second blessing came when Rex began work in Mancelona. Winter was rapidly approaching, so with no other recourse, Rex applied for work at Mt. Clemens Metal Products. He was hired in mid-October. After repeated failures in his own business attempts, Rex was happy for any opportunity that would provide for his wife and children. He was willing to take orders. Evelyn was pleased. She needed Rex's help with the family, and his work was only seven miles away.

The third blessing, but surely not third in importance, was the gift of their fourth child. Evelyn went into labor just as an early coat of ice blanketed the road in late October. Rex had to drive far faster than was prudent for the conditions. He prayed hard and drove fast. His wife was ready to deliver, and neither she nor Rex wanted her to give birth in the car. Evelyn was taken directly to the delivery room when they reached Meadowbrook Hospital in Bellaire. Rex called Doctor Rogers, who lived only a mile from the hospital, but Delbert Rex, ever after called Del, did not wait for him to arrive. He was born well and strong on October 20, five minutes after they arrived at the hospital.

Another great blessing was that Rex and Evelyn's newly acquired medical insurance paid the hospital and doctor for Del's birth. They were amazed. Rex had worked only a week at the factory before Del was born, yet the insurance benefits covered pre-existing conditions and paid the bills.

Though he wasn't usually a successful hunter, Rex killed a large, whitetail buck during the November deer season. He exulted in the rare success, and Evelyn was extremely thankful for the meat to add to their table fare. The Southwell family, now numbering six, had a house, a church, a job, and plenty of food for the winter.

The children rejoiced when snow blanketed the earth in late November, clamoring to go outside. Evelyn would dress them warmly and let them go, even though she knew they would soon be at the door crying, "My hands are cold."

In mid-December, Kay and David went with their father to cut a Christmas tree from the swamp that hugged the banks of Little Rapid River about a half-mile from their house. Though it was windy and cold in the open fields, once they had descended the hill toward the swamp, the evergreen trees provided protection from the elements. Rex loved the little swamp, and its silence and beauty, especially in the winter, was astounding. This was where Rex had killed his first rabbit, and its wonders had never diminished.

At a place where a small creek trickled over the stones, the children listened delightedly to its pleasant gurgle. The children's enchantment delighted their father. "This is Rapid River," he said. "It gets bigger on its way to Torch River. From there, they join their waters and flow on to Lake Michigan."

In late afternoon, they cut a beautiful balsam fir and took it home. Part of the tree lay on the toboggan and the rest dragged behind, marking the snow as if seeking to cover the family's tracks. Many evergreen trees become Christmas trees, but only balsam smells like Christmas. For those accustomed to its unique fragrance, no other tree, however beautiful, can measure up.

While Evelyn and Rex decorated the tree, Kay and David placed small evergreen boughs around the house. Don carried a small branch and followed them around, but he held it tight, unwilling to lay it down. The children sewed popcorn onto strings and draped the strands around the tree. Their father had done the same in his childhood, and he delighted in sharing the activity with his children. For Rex, decorating the tree was as exciting as Christmas morning. Presents were neither large nor expensive in the Southwell household, but on Christmas morning, when the children pulled their gifts from between the branches their excitement could not have been greater. Evelyn and Rex appreciated receiving gifts, but their children's excitement provided them greater joy. Later in the day, they enjoyed a holiday feast of roast venison, potatoes, vegetables from their garden, and apple pie for dessert.

Pastor Frank Brower, from the Baptist church they had begun attending, had recently spoken of how God left a ram in a thicket when Abraham had a desperate need for an offering. Abraham called the place *Jehovah-jireh*, "the Lord will provide." In just the last few months, God had provided abundantly for Rex's family, and Jehovah-jireh became a regular part of his vocabulary.

That winter, Harold lost interest in the farm, and he moved away in the early spring of 1953. Even then, once the fields were bare of snow, Rex drilled clover seed in the two remaining open fields. It was the last field he would ever plant. With Harold's departure, Rex was left with the responsibility, though not sole liability, for the debts. Once again, he and Evelyn prayed for wisdom for the important decisions that lay before them. The only way they could pay the creditors would be to sell out their farm business. The bills were long overdue, and the bank demanded payment. They decided to sell most of the machinery and all the livestock at auction. Convinced the farm could still produce an income, Rex kept the biggest, though oldest, tractor and combine.

The sale was well advertised, and the date was set for early May. Rex assembled the machinery in an open area near their barn. Good machinery was separated from that which he considered worn out. On the day of the sale, the weather was clear and beautiful. A large crowd came to watch and buy, looking for a bargain. To Rex's astonishment, the junk machinery sold high, while the relatively new, more valuable equipment sold for only a fraction of its real value. The cattle and sheep brought a good, fair price.

Income from the auction paid off the bank loan, but Rex and Harold still owed large fertilizer and feed bills to Jenkins Brothers and Vernon Spencer from the Walker Quickie soil enrichment program.

Chapter 17

MOVING ON

Rex decided the four hundred and eighty acres he and Harold loved so deeply would have to be sold. He contacted his brother, who agreed they had no alternative. They decided to offer Vernon Spencer the entire property on the condition that he would assume their debt with Jenkins Brothers. Mr. Spencer would have preferred cash, but this was a way to recover what could have been a total loss. Though Rex and Harold had paid only three dollars an acre seven years earlier, they were receiving a credit of ten dollars an acre. With the price of land increasing, the arrangement would most likely be quite profitable to Spencer, so he accepted the offer.

Rex put the paperwork together, and the property the Southwell brothers valued so highly slipped from their grasp. It was a sacrifice neither Rex nor Harold wanted to make, but at least their debts were settled honorably. Their families had suffered greatly from their business failures, but now they could face the future with a clear conscience.

The livestock had all been sold, and there was no need for hay, so Rex allowed the clover to ripen on the four-acre field that had been planted a year earlier. When he harvested the clover seed, the resulting income far exceeded anything Rex had thought possible. The field yielded four bushels of seed per acre and sold for sixteen dollars a bushel, which averaged out to sixty-four dollars an acre. That was exciting, to say the least.

Rex planted thirty-five acres of clover that spring, having regained confidence that farming could be profitable. His excitement increased as he calculated how much money he'd get if he made the same sixty-four dollars an acre the next year.

When he told Evelyn they could finish the house next year, she was elated. During the years of hardship, nothing had been finished on the house, inside or out. Now Rex and Evelyn committed themselves to making one major improvement each year. Working evenings throughout the winter of 1953, they finished the south room on the second story, and it was known as Kay's room for as long as they owned the house. The next and largest project would be a bedroom for the boys.

Rex seized every opportunity to work overtime at his job at the shop—Mt. Clemens Metal Products, in Mancelona. He could never make up for his mistakes that had cost so much, but he would try to earn a good income from here on out. In the summer of 1954, no overtime was available, so Rex cut and sold a carload of unpeeled eight-foot pulpwood. The price was much less than excelsior bolts, but he was able to earn an added two hundred dollars for the family.

Rex carefully watched his precious clover fields, and they blossomed beautifully. There was every reason to believe the seed crop would be phenomenal, so when harvest time approached, Rex decided to buy a new combine. His old Massey Harris was not very efficient, and the new Allis Chalmers, with rubber-faced cylinder bars, was reputed to be the best option for harvesting small seeds. Rex was confident there was at least two thousand dollars worth of clover seed in the field. The new combine would cost a thousand, but that was only half of this year's anticipated income. "Besides," he reasoned, "better equipment could result in more efficient harvesting, making such a purchase more profitable over time."

Rex didn't question why other farmers hadn't discovered this marvelous opportunity, but he soon found out because when the crop was harvested, it was of very little value. Most of the seed was from an obnoxious weed called "catch-fly." The local grain elevator was willing to purchase the crop, but separating the seeds was slow and costly, and because there wasn't nearly as much clover seed as expected, the income was minimal. Neighbors had encountered the same problem and would certainly have warned him had he asked. Once again, Rex had moved ahead without seeking counsel, and once again, the price of pride was costly.

Rex was reminded of a saying their pastor Brower had passed on: "Don't enumerate your juvenile poultry until the proper time of incubation has materialized." (Someone's interpretation of: "Don't count your chickens before they're hatched.")

Rex had greatly improved the eighty acres he and Evelyn had purchased in 1946. He had dynamited stumps from old fencerows, and limed and fertilized the fields. He had sixty acres of hay fields, and the twenty-acre woodlot on the corner was especially nice. The property had become quite valuable, but it would have to be sold.

Rex reminisced on another saying that often had proven true in his life: "The best laid plans of mice and men oft go awry." Not one of his plans had come to fruition. His parents had struggled with setbacks all their lives, but had been able to make slow but gradual improvements in their farm and standard of living. Rex, on the other hand, was going backward, rather than forward; until now, he had failed.

Rex looked at his wife with love and wonder. Through all his failures, Evelyn had never complained. Apparently, she trusted him—even now. Rex had learned from his parents, "Never, never stop trying," and the lesson would now serve him well.

Through the winter of 1954, Rex worked diligently and faithfully at his job at the shop. He at least brought home a paycheck, and usually it was supplemented with overtime. His work for Mt. Clemens was exemplary and appreciated, but he looked enviously at other jobs in the plant. Men in the tool and die section of the plant were paid twice as much per year as he earned in production.

Occasionally, the company offered one of the machine operators an apprenticeship in the tool room. Rex coveted the opportunity. He took the apprenticeship test in the winter of '54, and again in the winter of '55, but each time the apprenticeship was awarded to a younger employee. Though Rex was denied the apprenticeship, he was offered an opportunity to work in plant maintenance. Maintenance paid only twenty-five cents an hour more than operating a machine, but there would be more overtime and less monotony. Rex accepted the offer.

In January, the Southwell children began yearning for a television set, often referred to as "a TV." Their friends in school often discussed programs they had watched the night before, and Kay and David wanted to watch them also, but when Evelyn said other things had to take precedence, Rex reluctantly agreed. Rex really wanted the TV. He didn't know whether his desire was for the children or him and Evelyn, however. When the song of the first spring robin was heard, Rex's thoughts turned to Excelsior Bolts. At the supper table, he thanked God for the food then said, "A carload of excelsior bolts would pay for a television."

When the ensuing excitement diminished, Rex continued. "You kids are old enough to help. Harold and I cut stove wood when we were your age." Though the children had no inkling of the amount of work that lay ahead, they enthusiastically said they wanted to help. The next day, Rex called to ask for an order. Fortunately, American Excelsior had either forgotten or forgiven Rex for the extra bolts sent before, and they ordered a carload.

Bark peels easily from aspen trees in the spring, and when the leaves opened, Rex and the children, from Kay at nine years of age to Delbert, who was not yet four, went every evening and every Saturday to work in the woods. Rex cut around the bark at the base of tree and started pulling strips of it up the tree vertically. The children then pulled the strips the rest of the way for most of the height of the tree. Kay and David could do this work quite effectively, but Donald and Delbert were just learning to work.

When he was confident enough trees were peeled to load a boxcar, Rex cut the trees, finished peeling the bark and cut the logs into 55-inch bolts. In mid-summer, when the bolts were no longer slippery, Rex took them to Mancelona with the faithful, old Federal farm truck. He loaded them in the railroad car, and when he finished, the family celebrated with a marshmallow roast.

Freight didn't move swiftly, and when a carload arrived at its destination, it wasn't always promptly unloaded. Daily, for nearly two weeks, the children rushed to the mailbox to greet the postman, looking for an envelope from American Excelsior. Finally the check came! Twenty-two cords of bolts had been shipped, and the payment to the Southwell family was twenty dollars per cord for a total of four hundred and forty dollars. It was enough to purchase a full-sized cabinet TV.

The younger boys had not been able to pull much bark, but each person had done what he could. The children had enjoyed working with their father and their anticipation had doubled their enjoyment. Now they reaped the fruits of their labor with weeknight programs limited to a half-hour during the school year, and Saturday afternoon programs, such as *Sky King*. Rex and Evelyn enjoyed the TV also. The weekly program *Hit Parade* was their favorite. In later years, the family watched *Lawrence Welk* together early Saturday nights, often peeling and eating apples, which Rex dubbed "an apple party." Rex and Evelyn were faithful to the *Lawrence Welk* program long after the children lost interest.

Rex was more and more satisfied at the shop. The family income was not large, but it was adequate. In the winter of 1956, the large upstairs bedroom at the front of the house was finished for the boys. The main floor of the house had been dry walled or paneled. There was much more to do inside the house, but their immediate needs were met.

Finally, in the summer of 1957, the exterior of the house was sided. Rex had felt it more important to finish the interior for the family than the exterior for the neighbors, but this made a tremendous improvement in the home's appearance. The tarpaper exterior had been an embarrassment to the children. Their classmates on the school bus often made disparaging remarks about it.

In March 1958, the automobile market took a downturn, and Mt. Clemens Metal Products was forced to lay off many employees. Suddenly, Rex's only income was a semi-weekly unemployment insurance check that barely provided for the family.

Chapter 18

SORROW

Grover, who loved children as very few men could and who loved his daughters-in-law as though they were his own, was diagnosed with incurable cancer just before Christmas in 1958. He had only a few months left to live. Grover had initially visited two doctors, complaining of a terrible pain in his hip. The doctors treated the hip without success, but didn't discover the prostate cancer until it moved into his hipbone.

Grover graciously accepted that his work on earth was finished. He only asked to live his last days at home. Dr. Rogers arranged for the family to administer pain relievers when needed. He warned them that Grover had only a few weeks to live. Grace, with help from her old friend, May Armstrong, cared for Grover until he was unable to do anything for himself.

When Grover's condition deteriorated to the point that he needed twenty-four-hour care, Evelyn and Rex cared for him through the nighttime hours. When Rex came from work, he ate a quick supper and cared for his father until midnight. Evelyn then came and stayed with Grover from midnight until morning. In the morning, Grace resumed caring for her husband, and Evelyn returned home to prepare breakfast for the family before Rex went to work. When the children were on the school bus, Evelyn could finally rest.

It was an emotionally difficult time for Grace, even though her friend stayed with her throughout the week. For forty-three years, she and Grover had shared every hardship together. Now, during Grover's last painful days, she could only watch and wait. Though they could not alleviate Grace's emotional suffering, Rex and Evelyn shared her sorrow.

Grover suffered greatly, even with the strongest painkillers. Dr. Rogers expected his life to end much sooner, but Grover suffered on until spring. On April 14, 1959, Grover's spirit moved to its heavenly home, and his body was laid to rest in the Coldsprings Township Cemetery. Snowfall had been unusually heavy that winter, and snow banks obscured the automobiles driving past when Grover was buried.

Grover's grandchildren missed him. Until his condition rendered it impossible, Grover had always welcomed them into his room, and his visage had brightened when they were near. He had provided all the skill and much of the labor necessary in building Rex and Evelyn's house, and even though his warnings and advice often went unheeded, his wisdom was gone forever and would be missed.

Rex and Evelyn now turned their attention to Grace. She had insisted upon caring for her husband whenever she was awake, and she was exhausted and had no desire to live without him. She was very lonely, but when the first robin appeared, Grace began to regain her vigor, and when the wild flowers bloomed and the leaves formed on the maple trees shading her house, she forced herself to move on.

Chapter 19

FUTURE FORESTS

A great part of the Midwest's farmlands was developed by clearing its forests, but by the mid-1950s, many acres of marginal farmland lay idle. Leaders in conservation noted that in the past twenty-five years, thousands of acres of so-called worthless land had been planted to pine seedlings as make-work projects. These were now valuable forests. Would it not be wise to utilize the presently unused farms in the same manner?

As Rex continued searching for ways to provide for his family, the federal government began paying to plant trees at a rate of twenty dollars per thousand, but pine seedlings could be purchased for ten dollars per thousand from the Michigan Department of Conservation. A clear opportunity for added income presented itself. Before long, Rex began searching for a tree planter to pull behind his old John Deere GP tractor.

While some people planted trees with a celery planter, it could not be used in most areas due to the thick sod and roots, but there was no commercial tree planter available for purchase in the area. Rex would have to improvise. He bolted a left-hand plow bottom to a right-hand plow to provide a wide furrow that would remove the sod and other top growth from the field. Next, he welded a small plow, or shoe, to come behind and create an opening three inches wide and six inches deep in the furrow. Though Rex's invention served its purpose, the job required two workers. One man drove the tractor and the other sat on a seat above two small tires attached to the back of the planter. He placed seedlings in the opening made by the shoe, and the tires packed the dirt tightly back around the tree roots.

With help from his friend Jean Cunningham and later from his sons, Rex planted nearly a thousand trees per hour. It proved a profitable enterprise for two men. Seedlings could only be planted in spring and autumn when they were dormant, but Rex managed to plant a hundred thousand trees each spring and autumn, beginning in 1958.[26]

---

[26] This continued for ten years, totaling over two million trees.

That June, Rex began working for a neighbor building a house. The income was less than what he made working for Mt. Clemens, but it sustained the family until he returned to shop work in August. Evelyn could at least buy school clothing for the children and enough groceries for the family

The summer of 1959 brought a resurgence of car sales, guaranteeing overtime and extra pay at Mt. Clemens. Previously, Rex had only had one week of paid vacation, but it was now extended to two weeks. He was once again happy with his work and his employer.

In previous years, the family had contentedly camped at a local lake for their vacation, but now they decided to explore Michigan's Upper Peninsula. A man who worked with Rex had spoken enthusiastically about Little Blue Gill Lake, located in an uninhabited area near Manistique. His fishing tales were convincing, and decided their destination.

It was a long day of driving, including the crossing of the Straits of Mackinac by ferry, but the Southwell family finally arrived at their destination. Once the tent was set up, Rex took the children out in the boat to catch fish for supper. They were disappointed not to catch fish big enough to keep, but they were all sure they'd fare better the next day. Before retiring for the evening, they buried the garbage so their little campsite would not attract wildlife. The children even picked up tin cans that previous campers had discarded.

During the night, David began giggling loudly, obviously dreaming. Evelyn awoke, and when David stopped laughing, she heard a noise outside the tent. She quickly woke her husband. Tin cans clanged against one another as someone, or something, began digging up the garbage. Rex and Evelyn listened quietly, and were relieved when the noise stopped. In the morning, they discovered bear tracks all around the tent. One set of tracks was quite large and the other obviously belonged to a cub. Evelyn said to David, "That bear must have been tickling your feet!"

The first task every morning while camping was to fix breakfast, as cooking over an open fire can be slow. Once the flames give way to bright red coals, the excitement begins. This particular morning, sausage and pancakes were on the menu. After everyone had eaten his or her fill, Rex began to gather the fishing poles, but Evelyn stopped him, looked into his eyes, and said, "Let's pack up and go somewhere else. We didn't catch anything here anyway."

Rex wanted to try the lake one more time. It had taken a day of their vacation just to get to Little Blue Gill Lake and set up camp. Yet Evelyn persisted, saying, "All you caught were minnows."

Rex was puzzled then a thought occurred to him. "Is that bear bothering you?" he asked. Evelyn always kept her family at the center of her heart, and the encounter with the bear was too close a call. Evelyn quietly confirmed that she was worried about the children, so Rex immediately packed to leave. How could he refuse this request? She rarely asked for favors, much less strongly insisted on it.

By evening, they were camped in a state park on a lake near Iron Mountain, and the children were swimming happily. Rex wasn't optimistic about the fishing, but if Evelyn and the children were happy, he was content. The following morning, the family made the trek to an old mineshaft, one of the most interesting local attractions. Rex enthusiastically read every historical marker they encountered, though the rest of the family was interested not a whit. Of particular interest to the whole family was the giant pump that had kept water from filling the mine and the ancient steam engine that powered it. The ingenuity and determination of mankind never ceased to amaze Rex.

The family's old army tent could hardly be considered state-of-the-art camping gear: there was no floor and only one small window. When they awoke the next morning, it was raining, and their blankets were soaked.

At noon there was still no indication the rain would stop, so the family devoured what cold food was available, piled the rain-soaked bedding, clothing, and tent into the trailer, tied the boat over them, and began the eight-hour drive home. The children were restless and unhappy. Other years, they swam, fished, and frolicked in a township park at Six-Mile Lake, only a few miles from home. It had not mattered to the children that they were close to home, for every evening there had been a campfire and marshmallow roast. This year, family vacation was a bust.

Rex felt responsible for their disappointment, but while driving home, Evelyn whispered an idea in her husband's ear. Just before they crossed the Straits of Mackinac, Rex stopped at a restaurant. It was the first time the children had ever had a meal in a restaurant. The inclement weather had driven many vacationers inside and the service was extremely slow. The children were hardly bothered as the novelty and excitement of the situation kept them entertained.

Eventually, a waitress came past their table and began to take an order from an elderly couple that been waiting even longer than they had. The lady insisted that the Southwells be served first, saying, "The children have been very patient and have waited such a long time." It was rare gestures of kindness such as this that Evelyn and Rex treasured and hoped to pass on to their children, gestures exhibiting the spirit of compassion and love of their savior. As far as the children were concerned, the unexpected treat had saved the vacation. When they were back on the road, they bubbled joyously until one by one they fell asleep in the car.

The following Sunday, Pastor Brower told of a youth camp held at Lake Ann each summer and heartily recommended it as a vacation for their children. Partly as a sop for the disappointing vacation, Kay and David were treated to a week at the Baptist camp. The children were not as affluent as many of the other campers, but they each had money to purchase one treat each day—a candy bar, a pop, or an ice cream bar.

Kay and David loved the experience. Games were available to all, and the many tetherballs around the camp were in constant use. It was a week of great spiritual growth that may never have occurred had it not rained on their vacation. Because of the spiritual enrichment and great fun, Evelyn and Rex made sure that all their children attended the camp from the earliest possible age on through their high school years.

In November, Evelyn went deer hunting for the first time. Thirteen years earlier, Rex's brother Harold had chased that buck from the Rapid River Swamp, and Rex hoped to do the same for Evelyn. When Evelyn and two of their friends had been positioned where the deer would most likely run, Rex walked the length of the narrow cedar swamp. A nice buck ran past Evelyn, and though it was her first hunt, she placed her shot well and the buck went no further. Their friends, who had hunted many years, rejoiced with Evelyn. Though one might kill many deer throughout one's career, the first is always particularly cherished.

Though Rex continued hunting for the remainder of the season, Evelyn provided the only meat for the table. Not long after her first hunt, Evelyn began getting nauseous in the mornings. She soon realized they were about to be given another gift from God. "Rex," she said, "I wanted to be sure before I told you, but we're going to be blessed with another child!"

Chapter 20

A FIFTH CHILD

E velyn and Rex enjoyed having time for their children. It had been difficult to care for more than their physical needs through the winter of 1958. The children's welfare took center stage in their parents' life. In late spring, Rex and the children planted the garden, and the children pulled the weeds and tilled the rows, though somewhat reluctantly. Evelyn guided, and sometimes chided, but the garden was well cared for.

In June, the church gathered at East Lake for the long awaited annual baptismal service, an important public testimony to the community. Over the winter, a number of young people and several adults had accepted Christ as their savior, and all had impatiently waited for the lake to warm. There was no baptistery in the church, but Pastor Brower preferred an outdoor ceremony. Kay's parents were proud the day that she walked into the water to be buried in baptism and symbolically raised to the newness of life.

At times like this, Rex remembered that some fifteen years earlier, during World War II, he had promised that if God would get him back on the ground safely, he would never refuse anything God asked of him. Though Rex had been diligent in keeping this promise to God, in retrospect he began to believe he often did whatever anyone asked, rather than carefully examining if it was what God was requesting of him.

Years later, under the ministry of Pastor Brower, Rex learned that he could not have an effective ministry when his objective was paying off a debt. He began to realize that even though promises had to be kept, serving God was a privilege. "Your reason for serving God," Pastor Brower had explained, "should simply be the love for God." Rex finally understood; God hadn't answered his prayer to gain his service, but because of his great love.

On August 20, 1960, Philip Grover was born. It was nice to have a baby in the house again. Kay and her brothers showered attention on him until their mother shooed them away. For the second time, insurance paid the hospital and doctor bills; the family was no longer destitute.

Tree planting had become a dependable source of income, and Rex contracted to plant a hundred thousand seedlings in autumn. It was a hard five or six weeks work, and it took up every weeknight evening and all day Saturday, but it was important to him. He was rewarded every time he looked at the growth of the trees from previous years' plantings. Money wasn't as critical as in earlier years, so the extra income was saved for the children's college educations. In September, the old John Deere GP coughed its last. With contracts to plant a hundred thousand trees, Rex had no choice but to replace it. He searched in vain for a used tractor to do the work.

Once again, it "happened" that John Deere had stopped building two-cylinder tractors, and a 1959 Model-430 John Deere tractor was available for only $2300.00. Though reluctant to spend that much money, Rex made the purchase and was happy ever after. He soon had the trees planted and the stove wood hauled and in the basement for winter.

Working for Mt. Clemens was no longer a reluctant alternative. He was with his family, their needs were being met, and he was happy to be consistently employed. Philip was growing, the older children were doing well in school, and Kay and David were even playing in the junior high school band. Much work was still needed on the interior of the house, yet the family was reasonably comfortable.

On November 15, the annual deer season opened, and Rex pulled his car as near as possible to his favorite opening in the Mayhan swamp and walked the rest of the way in the dark. At one point, a large buck walked in and out of several openings. Rex saw antlers, but they were awfully short, and the law required they be three inches long. After hesitating, Rex shot it and found that one antler was three and a half inches and the other was four. Surprisingly, while the antlers were only stubs, it was an old, old buck. When the venison was cooked, the age of the deer became quite obvious.

Christmas, 1960, was exceptional. Rex and Evelyn could purchase larger gifts for the children, and life for the Southwell family settled into a comfortable, if not luxurious, routine.

In late January, Mt. Clemens again reduced their labor force, and Rex was unemployed. This was the second lay-off in three years. Something had to be done, but what? While he knew God would provide, Rex never forgot that he was God's instrument to provide for his family.

Chapter 21

BACK TO SCHOOL

Sub-zero temperatures ushered in the month of February. Rex stoked the wood stove, thankful the fuel supply was more than adequate, and began to plan his next move. Evelyn and the children trusted him, and he was determined to find some way to reward that trust. When the morning temperatures again rose above the big zero on the thermometer, Rex began cutting stove wood for the following winter.

It was a half-mile walk through deep snow each morning, which was discouraging, but he told Evelyn, "At least it gets me out of your hair." Evelyn smiled, but said nothing. She knew all too well that an idle Rex was an irritable husband. He would be happier out in the snow than sitting in the house.

Four months had passed since Rex had earned a paycheck, and there was still no work in sight. Unemployment compensation did help, but even that would only be available for two more months. Rex had to have employment, and a new possibility came along. A big step of faith would be required, but he felt this opportunity was the answer to their prayers.

The father of one of David's classmates said welders were urgently needed at the Big Rock Point nuclear power plant near Charlevoix. If Rex could pass the welding test, good work was available. Rex had learned basic welding techniques while doing maintenance at the auto parts plant, but he did not have the faintest inkling of the skill required to pass the test in a nuclear plant. His friend told him Lincoln Electric conducted three-week pipe-welding courses in Cleveland. "Maybe that could help me," Rex thought. He immediately borrowed some money and enrolled in the welding course.

When the three-week course was completed, it was obvious Rex was not yet a pipe welder. Welding on a bench, as he had done at the shop in Mancelona, was certainly not the same as welding around a pipe, where the quality and appearance on the top, sides, and bottom must be the same. Since he had already committed himself and considerable money had already been expended, he decided not to quit yet. He borrowed more money for further training and after two more weeks, he was able to weld well enough to pass Lincoln Welding School's minimum requirements.

With his diploma in hand, Rex eagerly and confidently drove to Charlevoix's nuclear plant, which was still in the early stages of construction, and was given the welding test. Earl Coon, the inspector, was as kind as possible and politely showed Rex the welds that had been completed at the plant, then told him his work did not meet the specifications. Rex was devastated! He had spent seven hundred dollars he didn't have and was still unemployed. It was humiliating to fail, but he needed a lot more practice before he could hope to work at the nuclear facility. Soon his family's economic crisis was concerning him more than the failure.

Fortunately, all highly qualified welders in the immediate area were working at the nuclear plant. When someone was needed to weld the pipes in a school boiler room, Rex was hired. He did well. He needed to make solid welds, but they did not need to be as uniform as he had been shown at the nuclear plant, nor did they have to pass an X-ray test. Rex's work satisfied his employer, and other such jobs followed. He was able to provide for his family, and his skill as a welder increased with regular work and practice.

After Rex finished a job in mid-summer 1962, there was no other work immediately available, and their future was apparently quite secure. Evelyn and Rex began making plans for a family vacation. Ontario had just completed the road along Lake Superior's north shore, and the idea of a family trip combined with the promise of great scenery was enticing. Rex's mother, Grace, accepted the invitation to accompany them. It would be no substitute for traveling with her husband as they had planned, but a trip somewhere new would be welcome. The trip was relaxing and enjoyable. Soon after turning westward along the north shore of the lake, a beautiful beach invited the children into the water. No one stayed in the cold water long, but each fulfilled his or her desire to swim in Lake Superior.

The scenery was as beautiful as imagined. A number of rivers had pushed their way through the rocky area, forming a spectacular vista on each side. At one point, the family looked down from the summit of a rugged rock cliff and was amazed to see railroad tracks on a long slope carved from the rock.

Reaching the western end of the lake, they turned south through Minnesota and became fascinated with the upper reaches of the Mississippi River. Everyone, especially Grace, commented on the increasingly fertile farmland as they moved further south into Iowa.

Evelyn's mother, widowed some years earlier, had married M.J. Jones, a farmer in central Iowa. Their home was the next destination. While Evelyn and Grace enjoyed time with "Grandma Jones," Rex and the boys helped "walk beans"[27] with Grandpa Jones. They were all amazed at the cornfields, which were already as tall as mature corn back home.

The Southwell family left Iowa and enjoyed a brief stay with Evelyn's brother Bill and his family in West Chicago. While there, they visited the Museum of Science and Industry, which was a great hit with the children. After nearly two weeks, they were happy to be on their way home to Michigan. The vacation was fun, but especially for children, "there's no place like home."

Rex began working for Wares & Son, the largest plumbing and heating contractor in the area. His ability to "lay on" a nice looking weld had improved considerably, and Wares was competing successfully as a mechanical contractor. Schools and hospitals in the area often required new boiler rooms or air conditioning systems, and Rex went wherever his employer had a need. Soon he was known as one of the "steady Eddies." Not many construction workers were blessed with continuous employment, but Rex was. Most jobs were within fifty miles of home, so Rex could drive to and from work. He loved his job, was home every night, and the family was well cared for. The 1960s were by far the busiest, most exciting years of Evelyn and Rex's life. The four older children passed through grade school, high school, and went on to college. Each played in the school band, and the boys competed on high school athletic teams. Philip, the youngest, accompanied his parents to games and band performances on a regular basis.

When Kay graduated high school, she and her good friend Linda Holloway shared honors for what would have been valedictorian and salutatorian, had the school recognized them back then. Kay then attended Grand Rapids Baptist College, and Linda moved on to Cedarville College, in Ohio. Their guidance counselor frowned upon the decisions. His two brightest scholars were rejecting the state universities and choosing schools the counselor believed provided inferior

---

[27] An expression used for walking the rows of soybeans and pulling out the weeds

educational opportunities. While he undoubtedly expressed his honest fears, the futures of both girls proved the wisdom of their choices.

To help their children at least begin college, Rex and Evelyn established a pine tree nursery business. The money from planting and raising the small trees was substantial for the time, and selling the seedlings to the Department of Conservation and planting them more than doubled their net income from the tree business.

The nursery was set up beside the large family garden. The seedbeds, three feet by fifty feet, were carefully leveled and treated to kill weed seeds. Pine seeds, purchased from the Department of Conservation, were scattered carefully on the beds and covered with a thin layer of sawdust. The sawdust was dampened each day until the seeds germinated and rooted, and then the beds were watered as necessary.

Each child cared for his own row of seedlings, which were sold in the spring and autumn after two years' growth. The ten dollars per thousand the children received for the sale of the seedlings was carefully counted and deposited in savings accounts for their college education. Upon high school graduation, each of the children had saved enough to attend one year of college. Evelyn and Rex had helped as much as they could. If their children wanted to continue their education, it was their responsibility.

Through high school and college, when work allowed, the Southwell boys accompanied their father on his annual fishing trips to Ontario. Each year they portaged further into the wilds, called "the bush" by Ontario residents, to establish their base camp. Rivers and lakes were followed until they could go no further, then all the boats, motors, food, and fishing and camping gear were hauled overland until they could once again navigate a waterway. When they reached the point of one day's travel each way, they decided that was far enough away from "the crowd." Their favorite catch was the Northern pike that fought ferociously when caught. They never went without plenty of fish to eat or their legal limit to take home. For their father, it was the ultimate vacation, and the boys told stories of their fishing trips to Canada long after they were grown.

With his continued employment with Wares & Son, Rex was able to provide well for the family. He loved his work and almost always was able to come home to the family at night. The one flaw was Russ, the only foreman Wares employed that Rex could never satisfy. Russ was always nit picking about something. He and Rex were seldom on the same job, but in the summer of 1969, Rex was working in Traverse City on a relatively large project at the state hospital, and Russ was the foreman. He was obsessed with his authority, or so it seemed to Rex.

On all Wares jobs, it was customary to stop work and pick up tools ten minutes before quitting time, which was 4:30 p.m. When the tools were put away, the men went home. It might be 4:28, or it might be 4:35. At noon one day, Russ said, "No one leaves the job before 4:30." That afternoon at 4:28, their tools were all properly put away, and Rex and his partner, Cliff Gregory, returned to the job office. The other Wares employees stood in a group, impatiently waiting to go home. Rex and Cliff joined the group, looked somewhat contemptuously at those standing around, impatiently checking their watches, shrugged their shoulders, and went home.

After six years with the same employer, knowing he and Cliff did more work than any other crew on the job, Rex didn't think any ex-second lieutenant was big enough to put his idiosyncrasies above the company getting the job done. However, when he returned to work the next morning, he was given his paycheck.

From then on, he would no longer have steady employment, but would go from job to job with different employers. Much of the time, he had to spend weeknights away from home because of the distances involved. There would be more periods of unemployment. Though he was forty-eight years old, pride was still costing Rex and his family dearly.

Chapter 22

WEDDINGS

In 1970, Evelyn and Rex strove mightily to keep pace with the changing events in their children's lives. They had been interested onlookers and vigorous prayer supporters as they watched their offspring struggle through the financial and academic strain of continuing their education. Now, one by one, they moved into the mainstream adult life.

In early May, Evelyn and Rex proudly attended Kay's graduation from nursing school at Bronson Hospital in Kalamazoo. Then they hurried home to prepare for her wedding to Garland Jex on May 16. As Rex walked the aisle to present his daughter to her husband, he struggled to understand the significance of what was taking place.

Having four children under the age of five had been exciting, but it was hardly less exciting now. Evelyn and Rex traveled to Xenia, Ohio where David and Evelyn Hare were married May 30. They then hurried home for Delbert's graduation from Mancelona High School, which was sandwiched in a seven-day period between David and Evelyn's wedding and their June 6 graduation from Cedarville College, also in Ohio. Three graduation ceremonies and two weddings in less than six weeks only dramatized the excitement of things to come.

Donald completed his freshman year of college in Cedarville in the spring of 1970, transferred to General Motors Institute in Flint, Michigan for his sophomore year, and then transferred to Western Michigan University Honors College in Kalamazoo, where he would major in mathematics. Before beginning his junior year at WMU, Don and Glenna Hall were married on August 21. Even with the transfers and marriage, Donald completed his bachelor's degree in four years, graduating in 1973 with a four point average.

Their third son, Delbert, left home to begin studies at Cedarville College in 1970. Rex and Evelyn viewed the four empty chairs at the dinner table and agreed it was nice to have one child at home. They weren't ready for an empty nest quite yet.

In mid-winter of his sophomore year, Delbert and Gayle Lucht became engaged. Scholastics were not Delbert's forte; nevertheless, he finished his second term before entering the work force to prepare for his wedding. Delbert and Gayle were married on December 16, 1972 in Huntsburg, Ohio, near Gayle's home, and a short distance south from Cleveland.

The night before their wedding, a snowstorm of no mean proportion blew through the area and continued throughout the next day. Interstate 71 was blocked through Cleveland, and many smaller roads were impassable. Some guests were unable to attend because of the storm, but fortunately, the Southwell contingent was comfortably settled in motels nearby, so the wedding ceremony and reception continued, in spite of the wind and snow outside.

In just two years and seven months, Evelyn and Rex's four older children had been married and were living in homes of their own. It had been a hectic time, but now the parents were content to center their attention on their youngest son, Philip.

Evelyn purchased a beautiful twenty-seven-foot travel trailer when she received an inheritance from her mother and was now able to enjoy the annual fishing trips with her husband and son. Residents at camping grounds referred to Philip as their grandson, which he well could have been, but Evelyn remembered when Philip was a baby and the same mistake had been made. While lakes with campgrounds accessible to travel trailers did not produce the number or size of fish Rex had been accustomed to when portaging on the river system to remote lakes, the fishing was still very good. It was a pleasant trade-off to see his wife share their enjoyment of these special trips.

In the spring, an unexpected opportunity for more prosperous employment was presented when Ken Dowdy, a friend at church, said he was moving back to Texas. He offered to sell his welding rig to Rex and introduce him to his employer. A local oil field was being developed, and Shell Oil Company was contracting work at well sites to individuals. Ken had been a satisfactory worker and upon his recommendation, Rex was able to take his place.

God was providing well for Rex's family. Contracting work for the welding rig and hiring only one helper gave the family a very good income compared to other jobs. Rex sensed an opportunity to finally have a business of his own and established a corporation under the name Southwell Fabrication, enabling him to buy materials wholesale. He purchased oil-fired boilers for his home and his daughter and one son's home. When Calvary Baptist Church in Kalkaska, where Rex was a member, constructed a new facility the following year, he also purchased materials for the church heating system and was able to donate the labor to install them. He was content.

While he could drive to most work locations, it was occasionally necessary to stay at a motel during the workweek. A year and a half later, on one such job, there was a large open area, so with Evelyn's approval, Rex took her travel trailer and parked it at the jobsite the following Monday. When the Shell inspector made his inspection a few days later, he advised Rex the camper could not be on their location. Rex thought it odd, but he moved it—just across the road. That area was not under the jurisdiction of Shell Oil. The inspector's approval was now irrelevant, and Rex had obeyed instructions.

When he completed his contract for that job, Rex was not given another contract. He didn't understand. All his employers had been satisfied with the quality and quantity of his work. Why had he been terminated? Only after a few days did Rex realize what he had done. The job locations were the inspector's responsibility and the work was under his jurisdiction. He decided who received contracts. Work for his welding rig and helper was no longer available.

Rex's desire throughout life had been to have a business of his own, but this was not to be. The corporation was dissolved. He would still have work in the oil field, but making substantially less income. Surely, he could be content to take orders from others, as before. It was a bitter reflection for Rex. Some learn slowly, and others never learn.

Chapter 23

WINDING DOWN

E mployment through the 1970s was kind to Rex. For Evelyn, the decade had ushered in increasing arthritis, especially during the cold winter months. Though she suffered physically, she continued to accompany Rex to all Philip's football games and other school events. Excitement peaked when, in 1977, during Philip's senior year, Mancelona High School's football team reached the quarterfinals in the state playoffs. Though an excellent team from the Upper Peninsula defeated them, it was a big occasion for the school and town.

David and Evelyn had begun serving as missionaries in São Paulo, Brazil in 1975 and invited his parents and Philip to visit them for Christmas. They jumped at the opportunity to see mission work in progress, enjoy some of Brazil's culture and scenery, and vacation in a foreign country.

They arrived in the mega city of São Paulo after an all-night flight and were met by David's family, and Don and Helen Hare, Evelyn's parents, who had been missionaries in Brazil since 1946. Their baggage didn't arrive with them, but they resolved not to let that dampen their excitement.

David and Evelyn took them to Rio de Janeiro where they visited the huge statue of Christ on the mountain Corcovado, walked the famous beaches of Ipanema and Copacabana, and rode the cable car to the top of Sugar Loaf Mountain. In São Paulo, they experienced the Brazilian churrasco rodízio where delicious meats were cut from spits until the diner could eat no more. They visited an outdoor market and were amazed at the quantity and variety of fruits and vegetables, as well as the flies swarming over the fresh meats.

The high point of the visit was the church service of the new church. It was held at João and Rute Pereira's home in their "back yard," a tiled courtyard about fifteen feet by twenty-five feet. The service was in Portuguese, but the hymns sung had familiar melodies from back home. It was a joy to worship God with people of a different language, culture, and nationality. When Rex, Evelyn, and Philip returned to Michigan after New Year's Day, they had a much better understanding of the blessings and obstacles for missionaries working in a foreign land.

The following Christmas, Grace, Rex's mother, joined the three travelers on a trip to El Jobean, Florida to observe Christmas Day with Grace's cousin, Fred Williams, and his wife Florence, whom Grace had lived near in her early married years. They went north to Piscataway, NJ to celebrate New Year's with Donald and Glenna, and then home.

That visit to Florida enhanced their life for many years to come, for near Fred's place were three empty lots on a canal opening into the mouth of the Myakka River near Charlotte Harbor. It was precisely where Rex and Evelyn wanted a retirement home. They contacted the owner and purchased the lots a short time later.

Evelyn and Rex had been gratified that their five children, one by one, decided to attend Christian colleges. Now, all their children were married or in college, so Rex and Evelyn were able to plan winter vacations at their convenience. With relatives in Florida, their son Donald in Houston, friends in El Paso, Texas and Black Canyon City, Arizona, they received many invitations to escape the cold Michigan winters.

Rex seized every opportunity to work overtime in the late 70s and early 80s, and he and Evelyn began to visualize one day joining other "snowbirds" in their annual winter trek to Florida.

After graduating Cedarville College, Philip married Kimberly Payton on June 12, 1982, in Westbrook, Ohio. When he began work for Shell Oil Company on a drilling platform between Los Angeles and Catalina Island, Rex and Evelyn's youngest child and wife settled far from their parents. In the 1930s, when Rex and Evelyn had finished school, employment was hard to find, so they agreed they would prefer to have their children move away and be employed, rather than live close to home with no opportunity for work. Also, since Rex was nearing retirement age, visiting their scattered family from time to time should be possible.

In 1983, there was no oil field work in the area, and Rex searched in vain for other employment. In the past, he had enjoyed construction work and wanted to continue working in the building trades until he was sixty-five. Two more years would add considerably to his Social Security income and pension, but that year, the only work available was on a huge powerhouse in Glenn Lake, N.Y. In earlier years, Rex had worked away from home much of the time, but then Evelyn had children at home. Rex did not want to leave her alone, and would not even suggest they try to find housing near a mammoth construction project.

In mid-summer, Rex and Evelyn counted their savings and esti-mated what their retirement income would be if they took retirement that year. They agreed they were far better off at sixty-three with the option to retire, than those who were a few years younger and couldn't find work. In addition, Grace had begun receiving 25% of the royalties from an oil well drilled adjacent to her property and generously divided the income with Rex and Evelyn. That provided the impetus and funds for them to have a home in Florida.

After celebrating Labor Day at home in Michigan, Rex and Evelyn loaded their travel trailer home with articles they would need in Flor-ida, filled the pickup with items Fred and Florence Williams[28] wished brought from their home in Elk Rapids, and drove to El Jobean, Port Charlotte, FL. They expected to purchase and set up a mobile home, but found a mountain of obstacles. A new survey of the property was required before anything could be done; individual permits for the building, the plumbing, and the electrical were required; the power company and water authority also had requirements to meet; building codes required the floor level of the home to be eight feet above mean high tide, requiring many truckloads of fill. Most of these were new requirements, put in place since a majority of mobile homes was set in their development.

Engineering companies were overloaded with work and said they would not be able to survey their property for some time, but Rex of-fered to pay overtime to get their survey done quickly. Management at Charlotte Engineering apparently understood the urgency. They sur-veyed the property during regular hours and did not charge the offered premium.

Rex applied for permits, cut the pine trees that covered one of the lots, hired someone to remove the stumps, burned the brush (after get-ting a permit to do so), arranged to have fill delivered, and rented a small tractor to level the dirt in preparation for the mobile home. The unexpected cost of permitting, surveying, and clearing the lot rapidly depleted Rex and Evelyn's funds. They searched in vain for a used mo-bile home that would meet their requirements then reluctantly acknowledged a new unit would have to be purchased. They were thrilled to discover a new fourteen by seventy-foot home could be pur-

---

[28] Fred Williams was Grace's cousin who moved to Florida.

chased for much less than they had expected and immediately thanked God for leading them in that direction.

In early November, the place was ready for occupancy, though the electrical connections had not yet been completed. Obtaining electricity was the responsibility of those who sold the mobile home, so Rex and Evelyn returned to Michigan to exchange the pickup for their automobile and to bring Rex's mother back with them.

They returned to Michigan shortly before deer season opened on November 15, and Rex could not think of leaving home without one more opening-day hunt. It was a pleasure he had enjoyed annually for thirty-five years. He promised not to hunt more than a few days, and Evelyn agreed. She would enjoy the meat from another deer as much as her husband would. God gave him a buck the first morning and a fond memory of the last year he would ever hunt. Just a few days later Rex, Evelyn, and Grace were on their way to balmy Florida and their first winter as snowbirds.

A stumbling block faced the family when they arrived in Florida. The electrical inspection had been done, but the power was not yet connected. With no other choice, they settled into their home for the night. At the office of Florida Power and Light the next morning, they learned it would be five to seven working days before power was turned on. Fred suggested Rex tell them his mother was ninety-one years old and would face severe difficulties if it turned cold. This brought the desired response, and power was connected the next day.

The first winter in Florida was a fantastic experience. Walking outside without a coat, daily sunshine, warm breezes, green lawns, leaves on the trees, and beautiful flowers were unbelievable delights. Grace reveled in the comfort, as did Evelyn and Rex. Evelyn thanked God for relief from much of the arthritis pain. She no longer had to struggle from bed in a cold house before the wood furnace could warm it up.

Rex carefully smoothed and seeded the lawn, then planted some small shrubs. Together they arranged flowers by the front of the house. It amazed them that common working people could share such a wonderful experience; it was like a dream come true.

The white Christmas, so traditional in Michigan, was forgotten in 1983. This year, they planned to send pictures to their children of tropical splendor, right in front of their house. However, Christmas morning brought a big surprise. It was twenty-nine degrees Fahrenheit! Rex hurried to sprinkle water on the flowers, hoping to save them from frost damage. At ten a.m., the temperature was still below freezing and the flowers were covered with ice. This was not the Florida they had planned to depict to their children! But they were not daunted. Rex put out chairs for Evelyn and Grace to sit by the ice-covered flowers in their heaviest coats. They then took the pictures of their first Christmas in Florida and sent them to family members back home.

Searching for a place to worship began in earnest. It had to be a church where Christ was honored and the services were inspired. They selected six churches in the area to visit before deciding which they would attend. The first church they visited provided a very entertaining service. A professional pianist gave a concert, and the music was beautiful. While Rex and Evelyn enjoyed the music, they felt acquiring a deeper knowledge of God's word was a more important reason to attend church.

The second Sunday, they drove to Punta Gorda to attend a mission church. The pastor, Jim Henning, was with Continental Baptist Mission. The simple message, the warm welcome from those in attendance, and the vision of a small group struggling together to establish a local church appealed greatly to Rex, his wife, and his mother. A call from the pastor and an invitation to join the members at Wilbur and Ellen Butler's home after church Sunday evening sealed their decision. They never visited the other four churches.

The newly formed group, which became Peace River Baptist Church, began construction on a building soon after New Years. The work was to be done by volunteers and supervised by Bernie Bishop, a builder with Continental Baptist Mission. Rex helped with the construction nearly every day until they left for Michigan in the spring. He had not been ready to retire, so working with other Christians on the church building fulfilled his physical need for activity and his emotional need to be useful.

Grace had become close to a lady up the street, and Evelyn enjoyed the company of several other neighbor ladies. The winter passed all too quickly, and upon returning to Michigan, they all agreed Florida would surely beckon when autumn returned.

Chapter 24

RETIREMENT

When Rex retired, he and Evelyn were able to share endless days of leisure together, just as they had shared evening drives together in the first summer of their acquaintance. "Surely," he thought, "retirement would be utopia!"

Back home in Michigan, Rex was free to fish, pick mushrooms, wander aimlessly through his beloved woods, or do anything else he desired, but soon he began to chafe. Fishing wasn't much fun alone. If there were mushrooms in the springtime woods, he couldn't find them. Admiring the trees that gradually replaced the barren acres where the virgin forests had been cut was nice, but the trees didn't change much from one day to the next.

Rex could have helped his wife with her work, but Evelyn really didn't want his help. The kitchen and cooking was her domain. She did it well, she had her schedule, and she liked it that way. Rex was welcome company, but she did not need his instructions regarding the rest of her work in the house, either. With the children all gone, there wasn't as much to do and she could handle it well without his help.

One consistent relief from boredom was the fresh outdoor air. Rex reveled in the brisk autumn mornings. After the first frost, the pungent odor of witch hazel permeated the atmosphere as he wandered slowly through the forest hoping to shoot a ruffed grouse. The autumn colors repeated annually, but he had been too busy to appreciate it in earlier years.

Previously, Rex had struggled to find time to cut the winter's stove wood. Now he had the time, but they needed very little—just enough to warm the house on chilly mornings before heading back south for the winter. The stands of trees were growing well. He and his sons had worked hard planting pine seedlings in areas useless for farmland. Now, less than twenty years later, their efforts were bearing fruit. Two noticeable changes had taken place. Once-open areas were now covered with healthy pine trees fifteen to twenty feet tall. This was expected. But Rex was pleasantly surprised to see areas that were once scrub hardwood clumps becoming healthy forests with a desirable mix of deciduous trees.

On one such walk, Rex suddenly formed a new goal for himself and the land. He loved the forest, and he loved cutting wood with his little chain saw; now there was purpose for both. Many acres that had been scrub forests before were now woodlots that needed thinning. He could remove unwanted trees that hindered good growth of others. The by-product would be many cords of stove wood. He was sure someone could use the firewood, but even if it were never used, the woodlots would be several steps nearer to becoming valuable forests in the future. That was his primary goal. Rex remembered how he and his brother had joked while hunting with their father. Grover had always seemed more interested in the trees than what they were hunting. Now he understood that interest.

The cordwood wasn't wasted. Rex cut wood for his brother, Harold, who was no longer able to do so. He cut wood for Delbert, who always had time to help others, but struggled to find time to get his own winter's stove wood. What remained was sold to Jack Standen, a neighbor. Rex was again content and fulfilled. In the mornings, he worked hard in the woods. Afternoons and evenings became more of a pleasure. He hadn't wanted to retire. Now, once again, he was doing something worthwhile.

Evelyn also stayed occupied, serving faithfully on the ladies missionary committee of Calvary Baptist Church. Each year, the ladies of the church made quilts for all the graduating high school seniors of the church. They also communicated regularly with the missionaries the church helped support. Rex was pleased that his wife was part of the nucleus of that group, for it was a ministry that interested both of them.

Evelyn was excited each year when she and Rex began their journey back to Florida. Though autumn in Michigan was beautiful, Florida's weather was much more comfortable. The couple often accompanied the neighbors to lunch at local restaurants. Together they enjoyed various television programs, especially *The Lawrence Welk Show*, which they never missed. Evelyn loved to crochet and soon had crocheted two complete bedspreads. She sewed a tribute to their grandchildren in the center of a wall hanging and sewed the names and birth dates of the grandchildren around the border. Though her legs became more and more crippled, her fingers were still limber.

In the winters of 1984 and 1985, Rex worked, welding broken and worn machinery for a contractor on a job almost directly across the road from their home. Rex felt a need to do something useful. He was well and strong, and the work met that need. Beyond that, the added income would enable him and Evelyn to purchase a boat, which they wanted very much.

Never having piloted a boat larger than the twelve-foot aluminum boat with a three-hp motor, Rex took a boating course offered by the Coast Guard Auxiliary. The instructor provided very little information about boats, but had an abundance of instructions about channel markers and regulations. Rex and Evelyn purchased a comfortable, used seventeen-foot tri-hull. They parked it behind their home in the canal that led out to Charlotte Harbor. Rex then built a ladder from the dock down into the canal so Evelyn could get in and out of the boat regardless of the tide.

The couple spent many happy hours fishing and exploring the shorelines. One beach on Hog Island, they believed, would be an idyllic location for a Hollywood movie about a remote tropical island. They marveled that there were so many miles of natural beach, most of which was covered with mangroves and unspoiled.

Rex and Evelyn were amazed at the variety of saltwater fish they caught. At that time, there was no size limit on most varieties, and they kept for eating whatever Rex was willing to clean. Evelyn was never a connoisseur of seafood, but she would eat it once a week if it weren't cooked in the house. They preferred redfish or spotted sea trout. Silver perch, similar to small bluegills from up north, were nearly always available and easy to catch. They were delicious, but there were only two bites in each filet.

They often made a surprise catch and had to search the Florida "fish book" diligently to identify the species. Small sharks took their bait occasionally, but they were able to land only one because their sharp teeth usually cut the fish line. When they caught a stingray, Rex purposely cut the line, wanting no painful sting from the barb on its tail.

One hot, sunny day, Evelyn was bored and suggested they go fishing. Rex was not interested. "There's no wind and it's awfully hot; it's not a good day to fish," he explained. Evelyn seldom asked a second time for anything, but that day, she wanted to go fishing. It was on that day that she landed a forty-inch, eighteen-pound cobia. They would never match it in size.

When their children and grandchildren came to visit, Rex and Evelyn took them for boat rides. Charlotte Harbor was also home to dolphins, which loved to escort the boat as it sped through the waves.

Usually, there was only one or two, but on occasion, they saw as many as seven. Their playful antics always intrigued visitors and were the highlight of the excursion. If the weather were cold or windy, they would take the families on a cruise up the Peace River or the Myakka River. The highlight on that trip was the many alligators along the riverbanks, some of them very large. It delighted Evelyn and Rex to show their family Florida's attractions.

Grace had enjoyed Florida for a time, but after three winters with Rex and Evelyn, she decided to stay in her Michigan home. Delbert and Gayle lived just a mile away, and they cared for their grandmother's needs while Rex was away.

David and Evelyn, and Jim and Carole Plunkett were the first missionaries sent to Portugal by the Association of Baptists for World Evangelism. They began work in 1980, and in April 1987, Rex and Evelyn flew to Portugal, where they lived for three months with their son David. Evelyn provided for them as though they were guests for the entire time.

Rex helped install water pipe and conduit on a new church building in Loures, a suburb of Lisbon. The walls of the Loures church were made of blocks, but unlike blocks in the United States, these were made of clay and similar to tile. It was easy to break holes through the blocks for the pipes and conduits. The electrical conduit was flexible and a coil spring inside the conduit allowed it to bend. The conduit could then be shaped to any shape and the spring removed. No bending equipment was necessary. Rex had very little way of communicating with the Portuguese workers but greatly enjoyed the work and experience.

Retail outlets in the area were small. Each morning, people walked to the bakery to purchase fresh bread. The customer carried a *pão*, a cloth bread bag, made especially for the unwrapped fresh bread. A neighbor made a *pão* for Evelyn, Rex's wife. Local bakeries also made and sold a wide variety of excellent pastries, which were extremely tempting. All too often, Rex and Evelyn yielded to the temptation.

When the pipe work was finished, David borrowed a tent, and the families took a short vacation along the seashore in Portugal. Fishermen squatted by their boats, mending their nets as in biblical times. Fresh sardines were grilled whole over an open fire as they came from the ocean. A diner easily pulled the skin from the sardine, removed the meat from the backbone, and ate it with freshly baked bread. The men considered it a delicacy, but both Evelyns spurned fish not cleaned and skinned before cooking.

During the trip, David purchased both goat and sheep cheese, which his parents had never before tasted. Shepherds tended their sheep along the highway and sometimes herds would block the road for a considerable length of time. Rex and Evelyn knew they were enjoying a picture of days that for the most part, were long gone.

Other sites also left them in awe. A small, beautiful, and aged cemetery, tended carefully by an equally aged man, graced the top of one hill near Portugal's northern border. Closer to Lisbon, one of the king's summer palaces was built on a big hill, or really a small mountain. It was beautifully landscaped and well kept. The road to the top was wet and very steep and caused the tires to slip at times, but they were able to reach the summit.

Portugal was a beautiful country. City parks were exceptionally clean and well maintained. There was virtually no litter anywhere. Rex and Evelyn loved spending time with David's family and seeing Europe. They were pleased to have been able to help with the church construction, but after the vacation, they were ready to go home to Michigan.

Chapter 25

AGING

There were six steps to climb to enter Rex and Evelyn's mobile home, and by the winter of 1987, Evelyn was finding the climb extremely burdensome. She agreed when her husband expressed a desire to build an easier access for her. They used the next few months to develop plans and prepare for an addition the following autumn.

Rex began construction as soon as they arrived in Florida in September 1989. After putting in many truckloads of fill, they hired a contractor to install a concrete driveway and garage floor off the end of their mobile unit. With very little help, Rex built a double garage, a twelve-by-thirty-six-foot Florida room on the front, and a back entry. While they still needed to install carpets and complete other finish work, there was now only a single step up from the garage to the Florida room and the rest of the house.

Rex added a garage door on the back of the garage, allowing them to pull their boat inside. It was a step they would greatly appreciate later. Both were grateful the outside work was finished when they returned to the cool spring weather of Michigan.

The heat in the summer of 1990 was oppressive, even for northern Michigan. Though Rex enjoyed thinning woodlots, he spent more of the day sitting on a stump "taking a five." Since he couldn't accomplish much in the woods, he turned his attention to making a canoe. David had built a cedar strip canoe in the summer of 1988 when they were home from Portugal for a few months. The forms were still in the tool shed, so Rex made good use of them to provide him with a summer of lighter work. When he was busy, he was content.

In Florida, November 1990, they laid carpet in the Florida room, installed blinds, bought two easy chairs, and installed an air conditioner. Evelyn loved the bright Florida room with its abundance of fresh air and openness. Her husband rejoiced with her in those pleasures.

When they returned to Michigan in 1991, Rex again enjoyed the beautiful summer. He could no longer cut firewood at his previous pace, but he enjoyed just being in the woods. The stands of pines they had planted and the hardwoods he had already thinned were a source of great satisfaction. In August that year, wild blackberries were abundant and delicious. Rex picked, and Evelyn canned berries until they had as much as they could use.

Rex hadn't been fishing in Ontario for many years and late that summer, Delbert scheduled time to take his father fishing, as they had done in earlier years. Rex was to gather the equipment and supplies so when his son arrived from Texas at five a.m. on Tuesday, they could begin the drive north. That Monday, Rex said to Evelyn, "I'll go pick a gallon of blackberries for you to use while we're away." Around ten a.m., he returned with both the container and his stomach filled with berries and began final preparations for the fishing trip. Before packing the truck, however, he had to stop to rest. "I don't feel so good," he said.

Half an hour later, Rex again began to pack, but immediately came back to rest on the sofa. Before long, he said, "You better take me to the doctor. This feels kind of like a heart attack." He had no chest pain, but his arms ached and breathing was difficult. Evelyn helped Rex to the car and rushed him to the emergency center in Kalkaska, ten miles away. By the time they arrived, Rex was vomiting and extremely weak. Evelyn's, "My husband is having a heart attack," brought immediate response.

In the emergency room, a vaguely conscious Rex heard the attendants say, "More nitro; more morphine." When a heart doctor said, "Call the helicopter," Rex realized his condition was serious.

During the whole episode, Rex felt no anxiety and told God, "Lord, if you want me home that will be fine. If you want me here, that's fine, too. Whatever you want I want."

Though few people really anticipate death, at that moment, Rex realized he had no fear of passing from this life to his heavenly home. He recognized God's hand in allowing the heart attack to happen in the relatively few hours between picking berries alone in the woods and driving to a remote part of Ontario.

Rex arrived by helicopter at Little Traverse Hospital in Petoskey, and two days later underwent triple bypass surgery. Recovery was slower than Rex expected or desired, but he eventually felt as good as new. His stamina was better than it had been in years.

Although it was later than planned, Rex and Evelyn returned to Florida that fall. A mission church had begun services only six miles from their home. They were saddened to leave their friends at the church in Punta Gorda, but they felt led to join those starting the new church. The area had been sparsely settled when they came to Florida eight years earlier, but it was now a populated community and still growing. They needed a local church of their persuasion in their town. Anything they could contribute in work or finance would be more meaningful to the missionary effort than in the established church they were leaving.

Evelyn's arthritis was getting worse, as was her ability to walk, even in Florida's friendly climate. With her more restricted activity, she and her husband continued to enjoy boating, but limited their fishing. Neither spoke of the coming changes, but both knew those changes would be necessary.

By the summer of 1992, caring for two homes no longer seemed practical. When Philip wanted to buy the home place, Rex and Evelyn were content to leave what had been their home for forty-eight years and become full-time Floridians. In November 1992, Rex began to worry that his wife might fall into the canal while getting into the boat. Since he was not strong enough to lift her if she fell, he reluctantly said, "I don't think it's safe for you to get in the boat anymore."

She agreed and said the pain negated the enjoyment of the ride. They sold their boat and gave the money to their new church's building fund. The church, recently organized as Berean Baptist Church, had purchased property and was making plans to build. To their surprise, neither Rex nor Evelyn missed the boat or the fishing, though it had been a major part of their life in Florida.

In January, Rex and Evelyn celebrated their golden wedding anniversary quietly, but Rex wanted to do something special for his wife. Evelyn's hands were swollen, and she hadn't been able to wear her engagement ring for some time, so he proposed, "I'd like to buy something nice, but I know you won't wear a ring or bracelet. Would you like a locket?"

Evelyn replied, "I've wanted a diamond for years." Rex was shocked but pleased with his wife's frank request. They visited a jeweler together and when they left, Evelyn had on her hand a symbol of the love her husband still passionately had for her. It was not a magnificent ring, commensurate with what Evelyn deserved, but it was far nicer than the original she had received when Rex was earning twelve dollars a week.

Later that year, on Memorial Day weekend, Delbert and Gayle hosted a family reunion in honor of his parents' fiftieth anniversary. It was the first family reunion since the children had moved into the mainstream of life with families of their own. In mid-summer, Donald called. "Mon, you have always wanted to visit Hawaii, and Dad has always wanted to go on an ocean voyage. We think we can provide both with a Hawaiian cruise. You can spend a week on a ship, visit five different islands, and then have a week on the big island with Glenna and me." His parents were delighted.

Rex did not understand Evelyn's reluctance to go to the bow of the ship at night and watch the moonlight dance on the gentle waves, but he enjoyed it immensely. The trip was all they had hoped for: breakfast on deck with unlimited tropical fruits, dinners in the elegant dining room, entertainment by a Hawaiian trio, a bus trip to the volcano on Maui, and a pig roast on Kauai. The visit to Pearl Harbor and the U.S.S. *Arizona* memorial added even more emotion and meaning to their cruise.

At the end of their first week, Don and Glenna met them at Hilo, on the east side of the big island of Hawaii. They drove together across the island, visiting another volcano along the way, and lounged for a week in a beautiful resort at Kona for a week. The trip was a great finale of the celebration of fifty wonderful years of marriage.

Chapter 26

SLOWING DOWN

When Rex and Evelyn began their first summer as Floridians, they missed the beautiful wild flowers and pale green leaves breaking out on trees in the northland. Even then, because they had started out as part-time residents, they quickly and easily adjusted to their new experience, appreciating the advantages of staying put.

The doors that had been installed so they could store the boat in the garage now provided an almost constant breeze through it. This enabled Rex to indulge in his woodworking on most days. He purchased a small bench saw and planer and began building canoes for each of his five children, with additions and changes in each successive one. Evelyn was pleased he stayed busy and especially pleased when he made cupboards in the back entryway with leftover cedar strips and fiberglass. There was little Rex could do for his wife because of her increasing physical disability, but when her ever-beautiful smile showed her pleasure, it was a great reward.

In the summer of 1995, the couple was driving north to see their children when Evelyn suddenly asked, "Rex, could you build me a grandfather clock?" Rex laughed at the suggestion. The only pieces of furniture he had ever made were end tables for their grandchildren's wedding gifts, but Evelyn was serious. "We've wanted a grandfather clock for years." That much was true. They loved the musical chimes and beauty of the clock cabinet, but the cost had always put one out of their reach. While visiting their daughter's family, Evelyn excitedly told Kay, "Rex is going to make me a grandfather clock."

Rex protested, "I can't make a clock. I know absolutely nothing about a clock. I haven't a clue how to make the cabinet, and I certainly can't build the mechanism."

Kay's husband Garland said, "Maybe I can help." He went to his workroom and returned with a catalogue from Klock Kit. "This has all kinds of clocks and clock kits," he said. The clock mechanism was about four hundred dollars, and plans were relatively inexpensive. Rex had never felt so overwhelmed, but he determined to take on the project. Evelyn was confident her husband could build the clock, but Rex lacked the same surety.

After arriving back at their Florida home, Rex ordered building plans from the catalogue and with encouragement from his wife began work. He carefully, fearfully, began to cut walnut boards his brother had given them. There were enough board feet to make the clock, but not if he made many mistakes.

Before long, he realized he would need a router and several router bits. To cut the curves he needed a band saw. The curves he cut were far from smooth, so he had to buy a spindle sander. The cost of the clock had now escalated far beyond what he had calculated, so he decided to make do with hand tools rather than purchase more power tools. He also began bagging groceries at Winn Dixie to pay for the new tools he had purchased.

By the spring of 1996, the basic cabinet was completed, and Rex had learned a lot and gained some confidence. Even more important, Evelyn was excited and encouraged. Together, they were sure he could finish the job.

Work on the clock was put aside when Evelyn received an invitation to a McVicar family reunion at the home of her oldest nephew, Jim Lotan. Jim and Ruth lived on a small ranch in the Bitterroot Valley, south of Missoula, Montana. The McVicar family was scattered from Michigan to California, and they had not been gathered as one group for many years. Evelyn's two brothers, Bill and Mike, were no longer alive, but her two sisters, Marion and Mary, planned to attend, as did innumerable great-nephews and nieces, whom Evelyn had never seen.

She could still get around with her walker and really wanted to attend. She and Rex had never traveled through the northwestern United States. This was a golden opportunity. The trip was long and arduous, but they always stopped for the night when Evelyn grew tired.

Driving through Nebraska and Wyoming was a highlight for Rex as it reminded him of the stories and heroes in the Zane Grey books he had read as a boy. In Utah, they turned north through the mountains and followed the Bitterroot River northward. Each new scene was a pleasure, and throughout the trip, they searched for small local restaurants where they could enjoy local cuisine.

Jim had erected a large tent on his ranch near a small, fast-flowing stream that made its way past the ranch house. Beyond the stream was a grassy field dotted with grazing cattle, and beyond that were mountain peaks. It was hard to imagine a more a more beautiful setting for the family to celebrate their time together.

Most of the McVicar siblings had never met the grandchildren of the others. After brief introductions, each generation settled into conversations and activities of mutual interest. Evelyn and her sisters were content to enjoy the comfortable setting and recall their youth. The older family members knew it was unlikely they would ever meet again, but those thoughts were not spoken. When the families departed, farewells carried with them a note of solemnity.

Evelyn and Rex's return journey took them east over the mountains to Bozeman, MT and later along the Missouri River for more than a day. They tried to visualize Lewis and Clark's voyage along the same route over a hundred years earlier. The trip was long and took its toll on Evelyn, but when they reached Lake Superior and the far western tip of Michigan, they were anxious to visit their children in Michigan and Illinois before heading back to their southern home.

Chapter 27

THREE SCORE AND TEN

In December 1996, the doctor recommended that Rex see an urologist. The news was not good. Rex's prostate was filled with cancer. Dr. Kub explained the options and asked Rex and Evelyn to carefully consider their decision. The cancer could be treated with hormones, which should give Rex at least five good years, or he could have the prostate removed. Surgery would result in a lower quality of life, and the results were uncertain, but Rex would probably live longer if he chose the surgery. The choice was theirs. Dr. Kub would not advise further.

Rex loved Evelyn dearly. She had been a wonderful wife and a great mother, but in recent years, she had become greatly dependent upon him. Rex now did all the housework and prepared some of the meals. No one knew how long Evelyn would need his care. His father had died a slow, painful death from prostate cancer, and he fully expected the same fate. Still, Grover's cancer had not been diagnosed until it had progressed much further. If God could keep Rex alive until Evelyn no longer needed him, it would be long enough. That became his daily prayer.

"Dr. Kub," Rex said, "if I knew Evelyn would not last more than five years, I'd go with treatment, but under the circumstances, let's do the surgery."

After surgery, Dr. Kub was mildly optimistic. The cancer was extensive, but it appeared to have been completely removed. Rex had no reason to worry, for a few years at least.

Each afternoon Rex and Evelyn sat under the live oak at the end of the canal and enjoyed the cool breeze from the gulf. Rex would peel a mango, or some other fruit they both loved, for them to share, but they seldom shared the same conversations they had experienced in previous years. Even still, the communion they experienced on those afternoons was precious. They were together.

In June 1997, Rex decided to replace the 1986 Plymouth. Since 1966, when he and Evelyn decided they would buy only new automobiles, they had purchased six new cars and driven each one at least 150,000 miles. The realization that this would be his last car was painful. He loved automobiles and each new one had been a pleasure. They chose a Chevrolet Malibu. It was the latest creation from General Motors, and they were confident it would serve them well.

That year, the annual trip north was a struggle for Evelyn but she enjoyed the ride. They both enjoyed the new car, and it was good for Evelyn to see the family again, but for Evelyn's sake, Rex was relieved when they were safely home in Florida.

Evelyn communicated less and less, seemingly by the month, but she seemed content. When Delbert and his family came to El Jobean in the winter of 1997, she pointed proudly to the gift for which she had waited so long—the grandfather clock. While the workmanship was not quite to Rex's satisfaction, the clock was attractive, and the chimes were pleasant.

Del immediately said, "If you want to make another clock, I have the lumber." Rex was willing to make another clock; in fact, he was eager. Woodworking had become a passion, and the garage had proved to be a handy place to work. Rex needed be near Evelyn, and making the next clock cabinet would keep him just outside her door. If some of the other children also wanted a clock, life could be both interesting and busy for Rex for some time.

The 1998 summer trip north was difficult because Evelyn now used a wheelchair almost exclusively. It was good to see their children again, but Rex was also thinking about lumber. He wanted to build something from maple. He and Del searched the woodlot for two quality maple trees. Though Del had purchased the property several years earlier, his father was welcome to whatever lumber he could use. They located the trees they were looking for. Del would cut it to lumber with his portable sawmill and take it with him when he and Gayle went to Florida next time.

Evelyn began to have severe problems in Michigan, problems that became even more severe when they visited Don and Glenna in Illinois. Rex grew concerned about getting her home. Evelyn never complained, though the trip was long and hard. Each time they had to make a stop, it was a burden for them both. When they saw Dr. Cohen, he said a stroke had caused Evelyn's latest problem.

That autumn, Evelyn suffered another stroke. She received therapy in the hospital and for a while after returning home, but shortly thereafter, she became totally restricted to a wheel chair. Rex was able to help Evelyn from her chair to the table and to her bed so she could stay at home under his care. Ellie Magill, Evelyn's friend and neighbor in Florida for many years, stayed with her when Rex went to the store or cared for other needs.

Rex was determined his wife would have proper meals. Though he had never cooked until Evelyn was disabled, he gradually expanded the variety of dishes he prepared. What could have been drudgery Rex accepted as a challenge, and the many hours in the house became a joy. Though communication with his wife was limited, Rex was happy to have her companionship.

Meanwhile, Rex continued making clock cabinets in the garage, checking on Evelyn regularly. He didn't think he would finish a clock for each of his five children, but he would make as many as he could. It was a joy when he could present someone a clock cabinet or other small gift made in his workshop. He thought of those as a glass of water God placed within his hands.

As the end of the century, neared, Evelyn and Rex reviewed the many joys that had been theirs. All their children were married with children of their own and serving Christ. There were twenty-one grandchildren and six great-grandchildren. They reminisced on past joys and had no doubt God would care for them through their remaining days, however many they might be.

At the breakfast table in mid-December 2000, Evelyn suddenly lost control of her arms. She could not feed herself. Rex helped his wife eat, but when she tried to move from the table to her chair, she was unable to do so. Rex called 911, and the emergency technicians came and asked if she wanted to go to the hospital. Evelyn said no.

The man kindly explained, "I can't take you to the hospital if you don't want to go, but you really need the care." Evelyn reluctantly agreed, no doubt fearing she would never return home.

In the evening, Evelyn appeared to be better, and Rex went home greatly encouraged, but when he returned in the morning, she was on life support. An even more severe stroke had rendered Evelyn unable to function at all on her own. Rex called all their children, and Kay said she and Gar would come down. Their two youngest children, Julie and Scott, could come, too, as school was closed for Christmas vacation.

When the doctor said Evelyn would never be able to care for herself again, Rex prepared to take her home. He loved his wife and wanted her to stay with him, but the doctor and nurses explained that Evelyn was unable to help herself at all. Rex could not possibly care for her.

With the reluctant approval of both Rex and Kay, Evelyn was moved to Tandem Nursing Home on December 22, 2000.

When Rex and Kay's family returned to his home, he looked longingly at the Lazy Boy chair Evelyn had occupied almost constantly for two years. "That chair will now stay empty," he said. Kay agreed. It was the saddest day of Rex's life.

On Christmas day, Rex, Kay, and her family were invited to dine at Tandem Nursing Home with Evelyn. Christmas was beautiful and sunny. Gifts, which had been purchased and wrapped some time earlier, were shared afterward alone with the family. Evelyn smiled during that special time. No one knew what was in Evelyn's thoughts, but God had given her a happy childhood, a loving husband, five children, and a number of grandchildren. Even after years of pain and disability, she could smile.

Rex had asked God to give him strength to care for Evelyn as long as she needed him. Surely, she needed him now. She had virtually no control over her limbs and needed help to eat. Each morning, Rex drove five miles to the nursing home and gave Evelyn her breakfast. When his wife fell asleep, he returned home. At five p.m., Rex drove to the nursing home to give Evelyn her supper and stay with her until she was in bed and asleep for the night.

In that manner, the twentieth century, which had been very good for the Southwell family, came to a close.

Chapter 28

CENTURY 21

Evelyn received therapy for several weeks. Every effort was made to strengthen her legs and help her to feed herself, but to no avail. Communication became more difficult, and Evelyn talked less and less. Rex tried to engage her in conversation, but she seldom responded. Rex and the staff also took her to various activities in the nursing home, but she participated very little. Nothing seemed to interest her.

One day, Rex said, "Let's go for a little ride in the country." After obtaining permission, he pushed her wheelchair down the bicycle path and lingered under the shade of the trees. It turned into a very pleasant hour with his wife, so the outing was repeated almost daily. If the temperature was comfortable, they sometimes walked for a half-mile. Rex was confident Evelyn was pleased with the walks, but he still could not engage her in conversation. On occasion, when he asked if she wanted to go for a drive in the country, she said yes, but usually there was no response. To Rex's relief, his wife never said no.

Rex's wood shop in the garage at home became his respite. He made several end tables with caned tops and shelves while watching TV in the evening. Caning was an art he had learned while building canoes. Still needing activity, Rex was pleased to learn his children and some of the grandchildren, having seen the grandfather clocks he had already produced, wanted their own. This would occupy him for many years.

In January 2002, Rex wanted to do something special for his wife. Evelyn had endured the same routine for more than a year, yet had become known throughout the care-home as "the lady with the smile." In the previous year, Rex had become well acquainted with the staff, and now he spoke to the ladies in charge of activities. "Our wedding anniversary is January 17," he told them, "and Evelyn wants to give a party."

The response was warmer than Rex could possibly have imagined. Invitations were spread throughout the home, the dining room was decorated, Rex purchased a giant cake from the Belgian bakery, and the staff at Tandem Nursing Home served cake and ice cream to all the residents who chose to attend.

A young nurse's assistant with a beautiful voice sang two sentimental love songs. Upon returning to Evelyn's room, the couple was welcomed with a table covered with a bright red tablecloth, a bottle of sparkling juice, and small glasses. Through all the activity, Evelyn showed no emotion, but since she seemed aware of what was happening, Rex felt she had been pleased. That was his reward.

Life continued, month after month, without change. Rex knew from his Bible reading and study that "Christ loved the church and gave Himself for it." He also knew that was to be used as a model for a husband's love for his wife. He was determined and happy to love Evelyn by doing what he could for her.

On the morning of June 16, 2002, Rex received an urgent call from the nursing home. "Evelyn is in trouble. Hurry. It's urgent." He arrived to find Evelyn in a coma. Her labored breathing was the only sign of life. He called the children and had an email sent to those he couldn't contact by phone. Donald called the same afternoon. The conference he was attending in the Caribbean could go on without him. He and Glenna were catching a plane to Florida.

Evelyn's condition remained unchanged for several days. When Rex could not stay with Evelyn any longer, he went home to rest. Throughout those days of waiting, he, Donald, or Glenna was always by her side. One event, though heart wrenching at the time, Rex now looks back upon with fondness. Each time Rex left to go home, he asked Evelyn, "Can you pucker for me?" Though there was no other indication of consciousness, Evelyn always pursed her lips to receive the kiss.

On June 21, Evelyn pursed her lips for the last time. Early in the morning of the twenty-second, Glenna phoned the house. "Hurry over! Mom is hardly breathing." Though Donald and Rex arrived within fifteen minutes, Evelyn had already gone to be with her Lord. Donald arranged for Evelyn's body to be shipped to Kalkaska, Michigan for the funeral, and he and Glenna accompanied Rex to his former home.

While saddened by the loss of wife, mother, and grandmother, the family agreed the days together should be a time of celebrating Evelyn's well-lived life and her move to her eternal home with the Lord. David conducted the funeral service. He shared childhood memories of a wonderful mother and her faithful service to God and family. He then turned to God's word and pointed out that all Evelyn's good works would not have earned her a home in heaven. Evelyn was in heaven because she trusted Christ. Christ had died that Evelyn might live.

A week later, Rex returned to Florida alone. He looked longingly at Evelyn's chair, which had remained in place for the eighteen months of her stay at the home. The vacancy in Rex's heart remained, but in reality, his wife had been gone for a year and a half. He missed Evelyn, and he would have been glad to continue caring for her, but for Evelyn he could not grieve. His wife had suffered physical pain for several years and had not communicated for a year and a half. Surely, she was much happier in heaven.

Chapter 29

THE WIDOWER

God had answered Rex's prayer for health and strength to care for his wife as long as she needed him. Now with Evelyn's passing, Rex turned his attention to a book about the last years of old growth forests in Michigan. He had struggled with writing it for several years, and in the spring of 2003, he sent the manuscript to an editor. The response from the editor was devastating. It required much more work, and she would not be able to help more than she had already. She recommended he find an editor more familiar with the area and the time.

In June 2003, Rex visited his family in Michigan, and Delbert recommended he talk to Jeannie Nooney, a family friend who had worked on a large local history book. Jeannie agreed to help, but warned she would only be able to work on the project intermittently. With no other reasonable possibility in sight, Rex agreed.

Jeannie and Rex began working on a manuscript that would both tell the story he desired and appeal to the reader. Back home in Florida, far away from personal contact with his new editor, the work progressed much slower than Rex thought it should. Though he was impatient, he remembered Jeannie had only promised to work on the book in her spare time. "She must surely be a busy woman," he thought.

One major obstacle remained. Rex had named the writing "Exit Virgin Timber" because the decimation of the last old-growth forests was a result of human effort to survive the first half of the twentieth century. Jeannie said that title would never sell books, but nothing Jeannie suggested met with his approval. This obstacle was overcome when David and Evelyn visited Florida in December. Evelyn, who read remarkably quickly, ran through the manuscript and promptly dubbed it, *Tall Trees, Tall People*. Her suggestion described both the beautiful forests and the upstanding lives of those living during that period. Rex believed such a title would appeal to potential readers. When David suggested as a sub-title, "A family struggles to stand while virgin timber falls," the problem was solved.

In January 2004, Jeannie finished work on the manuscript, and it was submitted to Pleasant Word Publishing. The publishers designed an attractive cover to properly introduce the story. Yet several obstacles remained, and when Rex left Florida in the spring to spend the summer in Michigan, the book was still not published.

Meanwhile, another unrelated event counterbalanced the frustration with the delay of the publication of the book. While in Michigan in the summer of 2003, he attended the wedding of his granddaughter, Julie Jex. During a lull at the reception, Donald and his son Michael came over to Rex's table. "Dad, I purchased the forty acres your grandfather used to own," Donald said. "There are two residences on the property overlooking your granddad's lake. Michael and Fawn will move into the larger house down by the lake. You can come and live in the cabin on the south shore." Even though Rex was thrilled with Donald's purchase, and that the property and Southwell Lake once more belonged to a family member, Rex hesitated at first. He had lumber and tools in Florida and his woodworking projects to finish. But the more he thought about the idea, the more it appealed to him. It would be wonderful to be back where he had lived as a child, near where he and Evelyn had raised their family. When he agreed, Donald and Glenna began to repair and upgrade the house for Rex to move into the following summer.

The cabin Donald and Glenna had prepared for him when he arrived in 2004 was in reality a very large mobile home. A fifteen-by-twenty-foot addition to the living room had been added facing the lake. Beyond the living room, a two hundred-square-foot rustic porch and railing extended over the bank. The view of the lake was magnificent! Also, at the opposite end of the mobile home, an equally large master bedroom and bath had been added to the back. This, Rex immediately decided, would be his guest-room. The bedroom and bath at the end of the mobile home were adequate for his needs and from there he could view the lake he had so admired as a boy, and perhaps appreciated even more now.

Memories of the springs in the lake and the large school of bass that swam from under the log near the lake's outlet flooded Rex's mind. As soon as possible, he was rowing around the lake, living past joys as he surveyed the changed surroundings. First, he compared the modern aluminum boat to the wooden boat his grandfather had made. Granddad had built a flat bottom boat and pointed it at both ends for use with a paddle, rather than oars. Rex conceded the modern oars in oarlocks were much easier to navigate with, though he would have liked to paddle the old boat.

The clear, cold water had not changed. The springs still bubbled forth. There was nothing to contaminate the lake, making it still safe to drink its water. Rex was mildly disappointed when no bass swam out to meet him as he neared the outlet, and the old log he remembered had either sunk or been removed. In the seventy years that had passed since he loitered at his grandfather's place, some things would have obviously have changed, but for now, Rex was content to live in the past.

The thrill of being at the summer home had hardly begun to fade when word arrived that copies of *Tall Trees, Tall People* were finally available from the publisher. Rex immediately ordered three hundred copies. Half were already promised to buyers, and he was confident that local bookstores would welcome an equal amount to their shelves. It was a history of the area, and those who read the story found it interesting.

Compliments and best wishes poured in by phone and mail from family and friends who had received their copies of the book. Rex was excited. He sent copies to Midwest Book Review, who rated the book excellent. He sent copies to the purchasing departments of larger bookstores. He visited smaller bookstores in the area, giving copies to the proprietors. In later compilation, he found he had donated approximately sixty books to bookstores. He waited in vain for results. Rex was puzzled. He was sure the book would sell, but no stores ordered copies.

He had given a copy to Island Book Store in Mackinac City. They operated a store both in Mackinac City and on Mackinac Island and had books by many authors on various aspects of Michigan History. When Rex returned a month later, he was told, "I enjoyed your book; my parents are reading it now." That conversation somehow awakened him to the problem: bookstores stocked their shelves with books by known authors. They had no confidence a book would sell unless the author had a record of previous success. Many bookstore owners had never even looked at the copies he had given them.

Instead of giving up, Rex scrutinized other possibilities for marketing his book. He donated books to libraries in all the nearby towns and villages. He sent a book to the editor of *Michigan Magazine*. He sent other copies to local radio stations. He visited local historical societies and attended senior citizen dinners within a reasonable driving distance.

Over the next months and years, Rex began to reap some reward from his work and contacts. In the two towns where he was known, Mancelona and Kalkaska, Rex was allowed to speak about his book at historical societies and senior citizen dinners. In each case, the demand for books far exceeded his highest expectations. However, it still remained a puzzle and disappointment to him why other towns in the area would not respond to his offer to present *Tall Trees, Tall People* to their membership.

Three major developments helped spread distribution to a wider area. His grandson, Jason Southwell, set up a web site, through which anyone could order books and pay by credit card. *Michigan Magazine* interviewed Rex on his porch overlooking Granddad's lake and placed the interview on public television and in the magazine. Hartwick Pines State Park[29] invited Rex to present the book on two special weekends. Each of these developments sold hundreds of copies. Soon, many more copies were purchased because readers told their friends and many of them also ordered books. Without the web site, most of these purchases would never have been made.

A local convenience store on Manistee Lake offered the book for sale and sold over two hundred copies in three summers. Rex's daughter and sons offered the book to acquaintances in southern Michigan, Pennsylvania, Texas, and Illinois. All these efforts were rewarded; sales continued when readers recommended the book to their friends.

It was encouraging to record a thousand sales within the first fifteen months, and again when sales of the second thousand copies were completed in less than three years.

---

[29] Hartwick Pines State Park, near Grayling, Michigan still boasts virgin white pine trees and is home to a logging museum.

Chapter 30

WHAT NOW?

After another pleasant winter at his home in Florida, in May 2005, Rex returned to Michigan with renewed vigor. When Evelyn died, he had thought his earthly life was over. Now, in his eighty-fifth year, he was still remarkably strong and had learned life could still be meaningful.

The forestlands, which had practically vanished with the harvest of virgin timber more than sixty years earlier, were renewing themselves. The trees that had been saplings only a few decades earlier had grown, and the forests were once again beautiful. As always, however, there were individual trees that to Rex were blots in the overall beauty, absorbing space, sunlight, and moisture. They would never be useful for anything but fuel.

Prior to moving to Florida, the only heating fuel Rex had ever used had been wood, a renewable resource. Now there were cords and cords of firewood that could be cut and utilized, at the same time greatly improving the value and appearance of the forests. Cutting and hauling wood as in prior years was not within Rex's ability, but with a light chain saw, he could cut a little swath each day. If the families utilized the firewood, that would be fine; if not, the wood lots would still be better for his efforts. Each morning while it was cool, Rex began work with the little nine-pound chainsaw his son Delbert purchased for him. Rex enjoyed that his grandson or son picked up the wood to use in heating their homes.

There were balmy days that Rex idled away a few hours on Grand-dad's lake. The bass he so fondly remembered were scarce, but perch and bluegills had more than replaced them. He was usually successfully in catching enough for dinner the following day. The simple joys he had experienced in his boyhood again gave him great contentment.

The following winter in Florida, Rex occupied himself working on the backlog of grandfather clock cabinets requested by his grandchildren. He also used that winter to write an autobiography at the request of some of his children. But in what seemed to him a very short time, he was back in Michigan for the spring of 2006, and a repeat of the prior summer's activities was in full swing.

In June, Rex experienced an emotional downturn. His son David, who was editing "The Price of Pride," the name Rex had decided best fitted his autobiography, came to the portion of the manuscript his father would have preferred to have forgotten. As Rex worked with David to be sure events were as described, the memories these discussions conjured were not pleasant. Rex realized and gladly accepted the forgiveness of God and family members for his failures, but he could never forget the hardships his follies had created.

Then Rex received, among other Father's Day greetings, an email from David—an email whose timing could only have been orchestrated by God.

Happy Father's Day! Before church this morning, I jotted down a lot of ideas about 'hands,' as they related to you. A few of the thoughts I had:

- *As my Heavenly Father's hand guides me, so did yours.*
- *I saw your hands as big and rough and dirty. You worked hard to make a living for us kids, and although we may not have had as much as some, we certainly had a great plenty and no idea we didn't have what others had.*
- *I remember your hands doing dishes on Sunday after dinner—you always said it was to get them clean, but I suspect you also thought if Mom did dishes six days a week you could do them once.*
- *Your hands held boards when we pounded nails or cut lumber when you could have done it much faster yourself, but that's how we learned to do things, and if it's one thing your kids do, it's "do things."*
- *More than once, I felt the hand of discipline (which unfortunately, I needed), and I also felt the hand of help—like pulling me out of the lake in Ontario. (I got your fishing rod, but it was a foolish move on my part, dressed as I was, and you saved me.)*
- *I saw your hands do lots of works of service, like at church, or at "my" church in Portugal with the plumbing, or at Peace River.*
- *Later in life, I saw your hands care for Mom and learn to be a very good cook (and pie baker).*
- *Your hand held a Bible and taught many a Sunday school lesson after hours of study.*
- *Your hand also has written some great things that all of us kids appreciate, and which have made us thankful for you; it took a lot of work.*

There are probably many other ways I remember your hands, but please know that I am thankful for them and thankful that in spite of all the mistakes in life (you listed many in your last book) your hands did a good job of being a dad. I love you more than you can know, and much more than I can tell you.

Dave

With a better perspective, Rex continued to work in the forests, but another distraction began to occupy his mind. Donald had Granddad's lake cleaned out the summer before, and Rex noticed the island near the eastern shore was partly swampy, irregular, and unattractive. When in early September the rays of the morning sun were no longer oppressive, he turned his attention to improving the appearance of the island. There was an abundance of sand available to correct it, but because it could only be done with a shovel and a wheelbarrow, working people just did not have time to do the work. If there was one thing Rex had, it was time.

Rex purchased a shovel and borrowed a wheelbarrow from his son. He chose a small area to begin with, which could be improved with a reasonable amount of work. As it had been with his work in the timber, the little he was able to accomplish each day became noticeable by the time Florida again beckoned in November. Rex looked back with satisfaction on what had been accomplished and expressed appreciation for the strength God had provided to do the work.

The forest improvements made in the morning hours, the relaxing times fishing in the little lake, the birthday parties of great-grandchildren, and the beautiful summer weather was a pleasure through the summer of 2007. In mid-August, even though the sun could still become oppressive before mid-morning, Rex returned to the task of completing the landscaping on the island.

In October, the autumn colors broke forth in great beauty, and it appeared the landscaping could be completed by month's end, when Rex's summer in Michigan would be over. Help had been offered, but he really wanted to do the work himself. Besides, even though he worked slowly, Rex was enjoying every moment.

Then, on October 4, Rex stumbled, fell, and severely bruised the bone in his upper thigh. When he felt well enough to continue his work, it became clear it would be impossible. His dream of completing the landscaping of the island before returning to Florida was doomed. In all probability, he would be able to complete the work in 2008, but doubt crept in as he began to feel the effects of his eighty-plus years. Reluctantly, he asked for help.

On October 20, his grandsons, Michael and Chace, came on a cool Saturday morning and with the vigor of their relative youth completed the work in one day. Rex had hoped to accomplish it in three weeks! The following Monday, Rex planted the area with grass seed and reveled in the completed project. The result was a great reward for the many hours of effort. He could return to Florida, happy to leave the cold and snow, and anticipate the appearance of the green island, now named Evelyn Island, in the summer of 2008.

GOING SOFTLY

Quite to his surprise, Rex has mellowed in many ways, most of them for the better. His movements are slower, his responses more delayed, his opinions less dogmatic, his actions more considered, and his alarm clock ignored. There is less strength in his coffee, less seasoning in his food, less sleep during his nights, less exertion in his exercise, less interest in politics, less aggressiveness in driving, and much less impatience. On the other hand, there is more appreciation for family, more beauty in nature, more music in songs, more compassion for all, and more love for Christian brothers.

Though Rex is subject to the frailties common to old age, he anticipates winters in Florida where his friends at Victory Baptist Church provide for his social needs and he occupies his time with woodworking projects. He equally anticipates summers at Southwell Lake, where family is close and the forests offer plenty opportunity for activity. Rex has no fear or reluctance of "crossing the Jordan" whenever God chooses to take him home to be reunited with his wife and family.

THE AROMATIC ROSE

From their dear mother's life
Her children all know
Love pure, sweet, and deep
As a dark crimson rose.

May the life that I live
And the love that I show
Be as petals fresh plucked
From a beautiful rose.

May the memories I leave
When my final breath flows
Be sweet as the scent,
Of the late, dying rose

When my body is raised
From the grave here below
I'll be clean, pure, and fresh
As a brilliant white rose.

FAMILY NOTES

Rex is grateful to God for his children and for their lives and career choices. Their successes he considers a special blessing from God.

- Kay has retired from her position as director of nursing at MediLodge of Montrose, a skilled nursing facility in Montrose, Michigan. Garland is an assistant professor of electronics at Baker College in Flint.
- David and his wife Evelyn served as missionaries for thirty-five years with the Association of Baptists for World Evangelism with headquarters near Harrisburg, Pennsylvania. David presently serves as executive administrator for Brazil after nearly eighteen years of service overseas. They give general oversight of ABWE's ministry in Brazil, including care and encouragement of missionaries, planning, problem resolution, and training.
- Donald is president and chief executive officer of Unitrin, Inc. Glenna serves with many local charities and organizations while making their home available for visiting youth groups and others who come to the Chicago area.
- Delbert is senior staff drilling foreman for Shell Oil Company, overseeing the drilling of oil and gas wells. He has worked in many parts of the United States as well as overseas in that capacity. Gayle is a medical assistant and has worked for many years in the offices of Mancelona Family Practice.
- Philip is safety manager for Amerigas, a large distributor of propane with responsibility for most of Michigan's Lower Peninsula. Kimberley stays busy as a homemaker and home schooling their children.

ABOUT THE AUTHOR

Rex Southwell was born and raised in the home that his father and grandfather built in Kalkaska County, Michigan. He attended the Davis School, a one-room country schoolhouse one mile away and later graduated from Mancelona High School. After serving in WWII, he and his wife, Evelyn, raised their family across Davis Road from his parents, Grover and Grace. In his retirement, Rex has kept busy with woodworking, including the building of cedar strip canoes and grandfather clock cabinets. He is the author of a previous book, *Tall Trees, Tall People*, which received an enthusiastic reception and encouraged him to write the sequel. He resides in Port Charlotte, Florida in the winter and in a cottage on Southwell Lake in the summer, near the spot where his grandfather built his pioneer home.